NOVELS, RHETORIC, AND CRITICISM: A BRIEF HISTORY OF *BELLES LETTRES* AND BRITISH LITERARY CULTURE, 1680 – 1900

by

Jack M. Downs
Washington State University Health Sciences Spokane

Series in Literary Studies

VERNON PRESS

Copyright © 2023 Vernon Press, an imprint of Vernon Art and Science Inc, on behalf of the author.

All rights reserved. No part of this publication may be reproduced, stored in a retrieval system, or transmitted in any form or by any means, electronic, mechanical, photocopying, recording, or otherwise, without the prior permission of Vernon Art and Science Inc.
www.vernonpress.com

In the Americas:
Vernon Press
1000 N West Street, Suite 1200,
Wilmington, Delaware 19801
United States

In the rest of the world:
Vernon Press
C/Sancti Espiritu 17,
Malaga, 29006
Spain

Series in Literary Studies

Library of Congress Control Number: 2022939779

ISBN: 978-1-64889-577-7

Also available: 978-1-64889-476-3 [Hardback]; 978-1-64889-525-8 [PDF, E-Book]

Product and company names mentioned in this work are the trademarks of their respective owners. While every care has been taken in preparing this work, neither the authors nor Vernon Art and Science Inc. may be held responsible for any loss or damage caused or alleged to be caused directly or indirectly by the information contained in it.

Every effort has been made to trace all copyright holders, but if any have been inadvertently overlooked the publisher will be pleased to include any necessary credits in any subsequent reprint or edition.

Cover design by Vernon Press using elements created by pikisuperstar / freepik.com.

Table of Contents

Acknowledgements — v

Chapter 1
Introduction: *Belles Lettres* and Histories of the British Novel — 1

Chapter 2
Definitions and Histories: Novels, *Belles Lettres*, and Criticism — 11

Chapter 3
French *Belles Lettres* and the Early British Novel: William Congreve's *Incognita* — 25

Chapter 4
***Belles Lettres* Rhetoric, the Novel, and the "Horizon of Expectation"** — 45

Chapter 5
"Let me make the novels:" *Belles Lettres* Rhetoric and Novel Criticism in the Romantic Era — 67

Chapter 6
***Belles Lettres* and David Masson's Victorian Theory of the Novel** — 101

Chapter 7
Epilogue — 127

Appendix A:
A Romantic Era Novel Canon: Counting Novels in Beattie, Reeve, Moore, Barbauld, and Scott — 131

Appendix B:
Scholarly Studies of David Masson — 139

Bibliography	141
Primary Texts	141
Secondary Texts	143
Index	147

Acknowledgements

The archival work in chapter five was made financially possible through a Northwest University Pope Faculty Enrichment Grant which allowed me to travel to Edinburgh in 2010. I am deeply indebted to the library staff at the Mary Couts Burnett Library at Texas Christian University and to the special collections staff at the University of Edinburgh Library, the National Library of Scotland, the Johns Hopkins Sheridan Libraries, and the University of Washington Suzallo Library for their expertise and willingness to find anything I ever asked for.

Portions of chapter six were drawn from my previous publication, "David Masson, Belles Lettres, and a Victorian Theory of the Novel," which originally appeared in *Victorian Literature and Culture*, volume 43, issue 1 (2015). These sections are reproduced here with the permission of Cambridge University Press.

Thank you to Linda Hughes and Richard Enos for their support and mentorship; to David Elder, Jason King, Angela Gonzalez, and Moriah McCracken for their camaraderie; to Martha Diede for space to write and research as a new faculty member; to Jessie Fast for her excellent – and fast! – proofing and editing; to David Dormaier for his feedback about publication and marketing prospects; and finally, to my wife, Lorri, and our three daughters, for everything.

Chapter 1
Introduction: *Belles Lettres* and Histories of the British Novel

> *I shall depend on you for encouragement when deserved, – correction where I am mistaken, and allowance where wanted . . . If I skim over the subject lightly it will be doing nothing; and if I am too minute I may grow dull and tedious, and tire my hearers.*
>
> Clara Reeve, The Progress of Romance

Most histories of the novel begin with an investigation of origins: Ian Watt ponders the significance of Defoe, Richardson, and Fielding as progenitors of the British novel (Watt 9); Michael McKeon peers into seventeenth-century French prose fiction (McKeon, *The Origins of the English Novel* 25); Patricia Meyer Spacks begins with the profusion of British prose fiction of the early eighteenth-century (Spacks 2–3). Yet rather than starting with a search for the origins of the novel, I propose to begin *in media res*, two centuries, more or less, after the emergence of the earliest examples of what would come to be known as the British novel. For this history of the intertwined relationship among British novels, eighteenth-century *belles lettres* rhetoric, and Victorian novel criticism, I will begin in an unlikely place: the servant's quarters of the Verinder household, with Gabriel Betteredge, House Steward to Lady Julia Verinder.

Betteredge is the first narrator in *The Moonstone*, Wilkie Collins' 1868 detective novel, and through his eyes the reader is first introduced to Collins' wide cast of characters; through his thoughts and actions, the mystery of the Moonstone is first unfolded against the backdrop of life in the country manor of an aristocratic Victorian family. Betteredge is the model of an unflappable English butler: his concern for the reputation of the Verinder family is the driving force behind his approach to relating the mystery to his audience. His calm, unruffled, and (mostly) dispassionate demeanor provide the perfect entry to understanding the various subplots and undercurrents in the Verinder household. But in private moments, when Betteredge is shaken by a new revelation or one of Detective Cuff's clever insinuations, Betteredge retreats from the family and takes solace in his pipe and a particular book:

> I have found it my friend in need in all the necessities of this mortal life. When my spirits are bad – *Robinson Crusoe*. When I want advice –

> *Robinson Crusoe*. In past times, when my wife plagued me; in present times, when I have had a drop too much – *Robinson Crusoe*. I have worn out six *Robinson Crusoes* with hard work in my service. On my Lady's last birthday she gave me a seventh. I took a drop too much on the strength of it; and *Robinson Crusoe* put me right again. Price four shillings and a sixpence, bound in blue, with a picture into the bargain. (Collins, 61)

Betteredge's tribute to the restorative qualities of *Robinson Crusoe* may seem a bit out of place in a literary history: as Betteredge says of his own narrative approach, "I seem to be wandering off in search of Lord knows what, Lord knows where" (Collins 61). But even if Betteredge seems unsure of *Robinson Crusoe*'s place within his narrative of the Moonstone, the house steward's relationship to Defoe's novel is an excellent place to begin examining the history of the relationship among British novels, *belles lettres* rhetoric, and novel criticism.

Betteredge's ode to the consolations of Defoe is hardly singular within Victorian fiction. Nearly two decades earlier, Dickens' David Copperfield found comfort in a host of early British novels, including *Roderick Random*, *Peregrine Pickle*, *Humphrey Clinker*, *Tom Jones*, *The Vicar of Wakefield*, and *Robinson Crusoe*[1] (Dickens 53). Little David Copperfield, at the mercy of the cruel Murdstone household, turns to early British novels to stave off the effects of his potentially damaging early childhood. David credits these novels with his salvation, claiming that the suffocating influence of the Murdstones would have left him "almost stupefied but for one circumstance" (Dickens 52). That circumstance was his father's collection of early British novels:

> From that blessed little room, Roderick Random, Peregrine Pickle, Humphrey Clinker, Tom Jones, The Vicar of Wakefield, Don Quixote, Gil Blas, and Robinson Crusoe, came out, a glorious host, to keep me company. They kept alive my fancy, and my hope of something beyond that place and time . . . and did me no harm; for whatever harm was in some of them was not there for me . . . This was my only and my constant comfort. (Dickens 53)

David later drives the point home even more dramatically, when he claims that his time spent reading was time spent "reading as if for life" (Dickens 53). Like Betteredge, young David Copperfield turns to novels – and specifically early British novels – when he finds himself in need of solace or comfort. The novels mentioned by Collins and Dickens are so firmly entrenched in the cultural milieu of Victorian England that the mere mention of these early novel titles is

---

[1] Dickens also includes the titles of two early non-English language proto-novels: *Don Quixote* and *Gil Blas*.

clearly intended to communicate a wealth of meaning and importance shared by the author and his audience.

The inclusion of these titles and the narrators' descriptions of their application in difficult times tells us much about the novel's progression from Aphra Behn's *Oroonoko* and William Congreve's *Incognita* in the late seventeenth century to the work of Collins and Dickens. We can see that the novel has become culturally instituted throughout British literary culture in a relatively short amount of time, between one and two hundred years. We see the novel as a vital part of the interior life of individuals, yet familiar enough to the reading public that no explanation is necessary to understand Betteredge's refrain of "*Robinson Crusoe*" or David's youthful exuberance in the exploits of Roderick Random or Tom Jones. We find the novel is part of the social, intellectual, and – in Betteredge's unapologetic declaration of the purchase price of *Robinson Crusoe* – economic life of Victorian England.

The rapid progression of the novel from the morally dubious and aesthetically ambiguous "new romance" or "true history" in the latter part of the seventeenth century to a genre so firmly entrenched – within nineteenth-century British culture, if not yet within the academy – that the mere mention of *Robinson Crusoe* carried significant cultural meaning is a story with a great many permutations. And while tracking down the immense range of influences that contributed to the development and cultural establishment of the novel is a task beyond the scope of this study, I seek to restore a largely forgotten or overlooked portion of the story of the novel. The social, cultural, and intellectual forces that converged to foster the emergence of the British novel also gave rise to a new discourse that shared many of the same concerns as the early novel. This discourse was recognized, by the middle of the nineteenth century, as literary criticism; however, as it developed throughout the eighteenth century, it was primarily known by another name: rhetoric.

The task of developing a history of the British novel requires the inclusion of a vast range of cultural, economic, religious, social, and aesthetic influences. But the role of eighteenth-century British *belles lettres* rhetorical theory in the emergence of the novel – and the critical discourse surrounding that emergence – has often been neglected or forgotten. The influence of *belles lettres* rhetorical theory in the development of the British novel is undeniable, and changes to rhetorical theory in Britain during the eighteenth century went on to shape the critical aesthetic discourse about the novel in Victorian Britain. This study makes the case for the direct influence of eighteenth-century *belles lettres* rhetoric on the novel and its critical reception in Victorian Britain and argues that eighteenth-century belletristic rhetorical theory played a key role in developing a horizon of expectation concerning the nature and purpose of the novel that extended well into the nineteenth century. There is a connection between the emergence of the British novel, eighteenth-century British rhetorical theory, and Victorian novel criticism that has been overlooked or lost; this study recovers and articulates that connection.

The character and shape of the early British novel, its development throughout the eighteenth century, and its subsequent rise to prominence in Victorian literary culture is a well-told if not universally agreed upon story, usually focusing on the novel's emphasis on the commonplace and everyday, on the individual and specific, and on the interiority of fully realized characters rather than the external exploits of archetypes and allegorical stand-ins typical of romance and epic literature. But little attention has been given to the ways eighteenth and nineteenth-century Scottish scholars and teachers of rhetoric impacted the progression of the novel and novel criticism in British literary culture. These rhetoric scholars, such as Hugh Blair and James Beattie, developed a rhetorical system intended to foster a shared national conception of aesthetic taste and judgment. Scholars of rhetoric have certainly investigated the importance and influence of eighteenth-century Scottish rhetoricians – including Blair, Beattie, George Campbell, Adam Smith, and many others – but this work is by and large focused inwardly on how these rhetoricians altered rhetorical theory or on how their theories altered the study of English within the academy. Relatively little scholarly work examines the effect of these rhetorical theories on literary criticism, and even less is focused on the influence of eighteenth-century rhetoric on specific genres, such as the novel.

Yet the relationship between eighteenth-century rhetorical theory and literary genres and criticism is important. James Engell argues that while the impact of this group is vastly underappreciated, their relevance to literary history deserves to be recognized: "The New Rhetoricians, properly considered a unified movement, are, prior to the twentieth century, the most important and cohesive group of critics in English" (Engell 217). If Engell is correct, then an examination of the influence of these rhetoricians in relationship to the dominant literary genre of nineteenth-century British literary culture – the novel – is worth pursuing. Ian Watt begins his investigation of the early British novel by arguing that the emergence of three writers the caliber of Defoe, Richardson, and Fielding within the same generation "was probably not sheer accident" (Watt 9). If I may borrow Watt's logic, the simultaneous emergence of the novel as a distinct genre at the same time as a new approach rhetoric concerned with taste, judgment, and propriety was hardly coincidence either. There is a connection among the emergence of the British novel, eighteenth-century British rhetorical theory, and nineteenth-century British novel criticism that has been lost or overlooked; this study attempts to recover and articulate that connection.

However, identifying exactly where and how the influence of Engell's New Rhetoricians touches on the development of the novel is complicated. The

Introduction: Belles Lettres and Histories of the British Novel   5

difficulty in defining the novel is a well-known component in the history of the genre, but rhetorical theory of the eighteenth century is almost as difficult to pin down. In their attempts to revise and refocus rhetoric, Scottish rhetoricians looked to theories of cognition and linguistics; they borrowed from advances in the sciences; they incorporated the work of philosophers and artists. The immense range of influences on eighteenth-century British rhetorical theory is daunting in its scope, in large part because these scholars and intellectuals give relatively few clear attributions to contemporary external works. Another difficulty is the sheer range of influence: a study of eighteenth-century rhetoric might lead to an examination of associationism, the Sublime, cognition, psychology, linguistics, genre theory, aesthetics, the history of rhetoric, grammar, composition theory, disciplinarity, morality, ethics, cultural imperialism, or a host of other possibilities.

Thus, examining the impact of British rhetorical theory on the development of the British novel – and the discourse that surrounded the novel – is perhaps beyond the scope a single project. Instead, I will pursue just one shared area of concern between the emergence of the British novel and the development of British rhetorical theory, one that emerges both within the pages of the novels themselves and within the body of criticism which quickly grew up around the rapidly expanding genre during the eighteenth century. Michael McKeon and Marthe Robert, among other scholars, argue the novel was the location where battles surrounding the cultural shifts of eighteenth and nineteenth century England were fought; I argue that revisions to eighteenth-century rhetoric – and particularly within what came to be known as *belles lettres* – made these battles possible.

Once again, I turn again to Gabriel Betteredge to aid me in explaining the complicated relationship of British novels, British rhetorical theory, and the aesthetics of morality. As *The Moonstone* draws to its conclusion, Betteredge returns to the narrative, first as part of medical assistant Ezra Jennings' journal entries and later as the final narrator of the mystery. Jennings' relationship with Betteredge is incalculably damaged when Betteredge discovers that Jennings has not read *Robinson Crusoe* since he was a child. This, in Betteredge's estimation, is a serious moral failing and one that requires the venerable house steward to re-evaluate Jennings, at one point telling the medical assistant that "[T]here are great allowances to be made for a man who has not read *Robinson Crusoe*, since he was a child" (Collins 430). In these few words, Betteredge, whose sensible, practical worldview centers the Victorian reader's perspective, sums up the importance of *Robinson Crusoe*. According to Betteredge, repeated readings of Robinson Crusoe are necessary for proper moral and ethical development; thus in Betteredge's view, Jennings' character and motives are severely damaged because he has not had sufficient contact with Defoe's novel.

For Betteredge, *Robinson Crusoe* occupies a place far beyond mere diversion: *Crusoe* has become oracle and moral code for the house steward, something clearly understood by the hero of *The Moonstone*, Franklin Blake. Blake, who has known Betteredge from childhood, succinctly points out Jennings' deficiency: "You have let him [Betteredge] see that you don't believe in *Robinson Crusoe*? Mr. Jennings! you have fallen to the lowest possible place in Betteredge's estimation" (Collins 430).

Jennings, a man of science and medicine, fails to grasp the importance of *Robinson Crusoe*, and Collins is on some level, of course, poking fun at Betteredge's reliance on Defoe's novel. But Collins is also making an important point about the position of the novel within Victorian culture: it is a source of comfort, wisdom, ethics, and morality for the Verinder house steward, a man of impeccable manners and propriety. Furthermore, in the words of Betteredge we can hear the echoes of eighteenth-century rhetorical concerns about the moral purpose and function of literature. Betteredge's reliance on *Robinson Crusoe* in times of trouble seems to echo Scottish belletristic rhetorician Hugh Blair's evaluation of *Robinson Crusoe*: "No fiction, in any language, was ever better supported than *The Adventures of Robinson Crusoe*... it suggests... very useful instruction; by showing how much the native powers of man may be exerted for surmounting the difficulties of any external situation" (Blair 423). This interest in the moral and didactic function of literature was one of the central concerns of British belletristic rhetorical theory, and the moral function of the novel occupied a great deal of nineteenth-century criticism of the genre. And while it is difficult to draw a straight line directly connecting the early novel to *belles lettres* to nineteenth-century novel criticism, it is worthwhile investigating the set of concerns shared by novel writers, rhetoricians, and novel readers during the eighteenth and nineteenth centuries.

In this study, then, I will tell the story of how rhetorical theory of the late eighteenth century centered the novel as a locus of controversy in the struggle between ethics and aesthetics in Victorian literary culture. I will build on the work of scholars such as D.A. Miller or Nancy Armstrong[2] (among many others), who have explored how the novel changed the way its readers understood themselves and their behavior within culture. In pursuing the relationship of rhetoric and the novel, I want to follow the interaction of the rhetorical concepts embodied in *belles lettres* and the criticism of the novel, with particular attention to the metadiscourse of the novel.

---

[2] I am thinking of D.A. Miller's *The Novel and the Police*, which argues that the Victorian novel acted as a sort of literary panopticon and also Nancy Armstrong's work in *Desire and Domestic Fiction* and *How Novels Think*, in which Armstrong explores the novel's effect on Victorian conceptions of identity, individuality, and gender roles.

Introduction: Belles Lettres and Histories of the British Novel   7

In *The Work of Writing*, Clifford Siskin observes that as any historically sensitive study expands, the subject of such a study necessarily comes to include the body of thought surrounding the subject: "as [the] database is extended *historically* the 'it' becomes, increasingly, earlier kinds of writing *about* it" (Siskin 49). Siskin's observation is particularly relevant in an examination of the novel: authors, critics, and readers of novels participated in a discourse about the purpose and function of the genre from the earliest stages of the novel's development in English; furthermore, this discussion took place not only within the periodical press of the eighteenth and nineteenth centuries, but also within the very pages of the novels themselves. Siskin argues that the early novel is, in its response to earlier prose genres, itself a form of criticism (Siskin 25). Thus, criticism of the novel, both as discourse and meta-discourse, is central to the development of the genre.

I argue that many of the basic structures for conducting and exploring this discourse about the purpose and function of the novel developed out of the collection of aesthetic and moral concerns systematized and deployed by the rhetoricians and critics of the Scottish enlightenment, particularly within the work of Lord Kames, James Beattie, and especially Hugh Blair. The belletristic concern with the intersection of ethics and aesthetics plays out within the novelistic discourse – and metadiscourse – of the eighteenth and nineteenth centuries, and it is this focus on the resolution of the conflict between the moral and artistic function of the novel I hope to pursue through an examination of eighteenth-century British rhetorical theory.

Necessity will dictate that I do not tell the story in its entirety: the intellectual milieu of the eighteenth century and its effect on the reading public and the development of the novel is an immense and well-trodden landscape. Instead, by purposefully maintaining a narrow focus I will be able to home in on the most salient texts, enabling a pursuit of the relationship between British rhetoric, novels, and criticism across two centuries. I will begin by examining the French origins of *belles lettres* and their relationship to the early novel, particularly within the pages of William Congreve's *Incognita*. Congreve's novel, I argue, is a transitional text: it is firmly rooted in classicism and the cultural context of the Restoration, yet Congreve consciously and purposefully deploys novelistic concerns with individual agency and interiority; furthermore, the novel's preface describes the purpose and function of the novel genre in terms closely related to French belletristic rhetoric.

From Congreve and French *belles lettres*, I will move to the development of Scottish *belles lettres*, establishing how Scottish *belles lettres* provided the structures for examining what Marthe Robert describes as the central concern of the novel, "the inextricable combination of ethics and aesthetics" (Robert 63), that I argue is one of the most important characteristics of the genre. This examination of Scottish *belles lettres* will focus primarily on Hugh Blair's *Lectures on Rhetoric and Belles Lettres*, delivered at the University of Edinburgh beginning in 1759 and first published in 1783. Blair's lectures are certainly not original in their thought, but his lucid and cogent systemization of the wide range of intellectual and aesthetic concerns of eighteenth-century rhetorical theory had a far-reaching effect in the nineteenth century. From Blair, I will turn to Clara Reeve's 1785 history of the novel, *The Progress of Romance*, and compare her conclusions about the genre to the work of Scottish rhetorician James Beattie, whose 1783 essay, *On Fable and Romance*, approaches the question of the novel's purpose from a rhetorician's perspective. The examination of Reeve – whose work is perhaps the earliest attempt in English to develop a cohesive history of the novel – will lead to a discussion of canon formation.

The contingencies surrounding the formation of the British novel canon is a complex and variegated issue, one that necessitates an understanding of literacy patterns, the expanding middle class, reading habits, domestic economics, the printing industry, and copyright law. In these matters, I will draw on the expertise of scholars such as Richard Altick, Laurel Brake, William St. Clair, and Clifford Siskin, whose work in these fields is comprehensive and nuanced. Rather than arguing for an entirely new understanding of the formation of the British novel canon, I simply hope to add another layer to the discussion by arguing that, among these other contingencies, the novels that became part of the canon were most often those novels in which the struggle between ethics and aesthetics was most clearly and purposefully evident. The novel canons offered by Anna Letitia Barbauld and Walter Scott in the early nineteenth century reflect an attention to the moral purpose and function of the novel that is firmly grounded in belletristic principles of literary criticism most clearly presented in Hugh Blair's *Lectures on Rhetoric and Belles Lettres*.

Finally, I will examine Victorian criticism of the novel, focusing both on the periodical press and the academy. A belletristic emphasis on taste, judgment, and moral content clearly resonates throughout the corpus of Victorian novel criticism, and during the nineteenth century the periodical press became the most important location for discussions of the purpose and function of novels. Much of the discussion of novels within Victorian periodicals revolves around the relationship of moral and aesthetic purpose. While in the middle and later Victorian era, critics like George Eliot and Henry James would argue that the moral dimension of fiction is found, essentially, in its aesthetic merit, other critics stridently argued for a specific moral purpose in literature, particularly in the novel. This insistence on morality as part of the Victorian critical literary paradigm is firmly grounded in the rhetorical tradition of the eighteenth century and can be traced at least to Quintilian, who infuses his rhetoric with a moral dimension in his familiar description of the perfect orator as "a good

Introduction: Belles Lettres and Histories of the British Novel

man speaking well." Hugh Blair greatly admired Quintilian, and the eighteenth-century belletrists' corpus reflects a belief that moral purpose should never be sacrificed to aesthetic perfection. The tension between the moral and the aesthetic was at the heart of much Victorian criticism of the novel: for example, in an 1861 article, Dinah Mulock Craik agonized over the moral ambiguity she found within the aesthetic purity of George Eliot's *The Mill on the Floss*. Craik's concerns about the influence of morally dubious, though aesthetically brilliant, fiction on its readers is just one example of the echoes of eighteenth-century belletristic rhetoric that took root in Victorian criticism of the novel.

As these discussions were taking place in Victorian periodicals, novels were also becoming subject to extended criticism within the academy. The study of British literature came exceptionally late to the Oxbridge schools, and when it did finally arrive, it was in the form of philology and the study of Anglo-Saxon literature (McMurtry 145). In the Scottish and dissenting universities, however, contemporary English literature became part of the core curriculum during the nineteenth century. Here I will examine the novel criticism and theory of David Masson. Masson taught British literature and rhetoric at University College, London, and at the University of Edinburgh, where he served as the Regius Professor of Literature and *Belles Lettres*. Masson was not just an academic, though: he was the first editor of *Macmillan's Magazine*, a prodigious writer of literary biography[3], and a prolific literary critic, publishing an impressive range of literary criticism in *Macmillan's*, *The North British Review*, *Fraser's*, *The British Quarterly Review*, and *The Edinburgh Review*. Masson's work, I will show, is firmly grounded in rhetorical theory and is particularly indebted to the belletristic rhetorical theory of the first Regius Professor of *Belles Lettres* at the University of Edinburgh, Hugh Blair. Examining Masson's commitment to rhetoric in his literary criticism brings the examination of the relationship between rhetoric, criticism, and the novel full circle as Masson explicitly ties his Victorian-era criticism of the novel to the rhetorical theory of the eighteenth century. But to begin examining how *belles lettres* rhetoric is related to criticism and the history of the British novel, we must first look to other histories of the genre to discover how eighteenth-century British *belles lettres* rhetorical theory might find its way back into the story of the British novel.

---

[3] Masson's multivolume life of John Milton was a foundational Milton text well into the twentieth century.

Chapter 2

Definitions and Histories:
Novels, *Belles Lettres*, and Criticism

> *Let me bespeak your favour, by assuring you that I mean to do something more than merely to investigate names: we will afterwards proceed to consider the beauties and defects of these writings, of the uses and abuses, and of their effects upon the manners of the times in which they were written.*
>
> <div align="right">Clara Reeve, <i>The Progress of Romance</i></div>

Throughout the more than six decades since it first appeared, the conceptualization of the emergence and growth of the British novel advanced in Ian Watt's *The Rise of the Novel* has exerted outsized influence on subsequent histories of the genre. Michael McKeon argues that the enduring centrality of this "rise" paradigm is a testament to the lucidity of Watt's argument (McKeon, "Generic Transformation" 382). In *The Rise of the Novel*, Watt describes a broad expansion in the reading public during the eighteenth century, fueled by the rise of non-Anglican Protestant denominations, the growth of the middle class, and the development of empiricist philosophical and scientific thought, as the three major factors that contributed to the emergence of the novel in eighteenth-century British literary culture. Though Watt's argument for "formal realism" as the defining characteristic of the newly emergent genre is by any measure dated and outmoded, Watt's model of the rise of the novel has achieved a somewhat monolithic status, spawning decades of critical responses that have sought to embrace, complicate, undermine, or discredit his assessment of the historical contingencies that converged to foster the novel genre's rapid development in the eighteenth century. For these reasons, *The Rise of the Novel* is often the default starting point for histories of the novel.

Yet as Lennard Davis observes, Watt is not necessarily the best or only beginning point for understanding the history of novel theory and criticism:

> Too often when we read eighteenth-century novels, we read them with the welter of questions of our own epoch. To focus on what novels meant to the eighteenth century, we have to pay attention to novel theory and the way it changed over the past three hundred years. (Davis 480)

Davis goes on to develop a history of novel theory and criticism that reaches back to the late seventeenth century, as the authors of what have become known as the earliest novels began to develop justifications for their particular variety of prose fiction. Often these authorial musings – in the form of prefaces, forwards, letters, or even digressions within the very texts of their fiction – focused on some of the criteria later developed by Watt and other twentieth century critics. Thus, Watt's conception of formal realism is not nearly so problematic in its specific readings of Defoe, Richardson, and Fielding as in its implicit and narrow assertion that the history of the British novel must begin with *Robinson Crusoe*. As J. Paul Hunter succinctly argues, Watt's focus on formal realism "diminishes the very idea of the novel and trivializes the conception of a literary species" (Hunter 22–23). For the purposes of this study, the primary difficulty is that the centrality of Watt and the criticism of the rise paradigm which followed has tended to obscure the important role of early criticism of the novel in establishing the novel as a legitimate and respectable genre in British literary culture. The rich and complex eighteenth-century assessments of the novel which influenced the development of the novel into the nineteenth century have often been sidelined as too simplistic or non-theoretical to warrant extended critical attention.

The failure to account for pre-twentieth century novel criticism in considering histories of the novel is specifically related to another problem: the role of British rhetorical theory – particularly as developed during the eighteenth century in Scotland – in establishing the intellectual groundwork for later critical aesthetic assessments of the novel has been almost completely overlooked. Robert Crawford asserts that histories of English as an academic discipline often "downplay or ignore" the development of literary studies in eighteenth-century Scotland (Crawford 1-2). In her dissertation, *The Art of Common Sense*, Lois Agnew goes even further and observes that overlooking the role of eighteenth-century rhetoric in the development of nineteenth-century aesthetic practices creates a gap in any scholarship that attempts to understand the progression from eighteenth- to nineteenth-century British literature and criticism. In particular, the belletristic rhetorical theories that developed in France and in the work of Scottish intellectuals, and which were later synthesized by Hugh Blair during the second half of the eighteenth century, had a direct and clearly identifiable effect on critical and aesthetic practices of the nineteenth century. Thus, a better grasp of *belles lettres* and other trends in eighteenth-century British rhetoric would provide a unique avenue for understanding the development of the early novel and the later establishment of critical aesthetic principles that influenced the novel's push toward literary dominance in the nineteenth century.

Definitions and Histories   13

But just what is a novel? A typical definition is offered by Margaret Anne Doody, who succinctly defines a work as a novel "if it is fictional, if it is in prose, and if it is of a certain length" (Doody 16). Terry Eagleton seems to agree with Doody's definition when he defines the novel as "a piece of prose fiction of a reasonable length" (Eagleton 1). Doody, in fact, attempts to completely dissolve the novel's genre boundaries, blurring the lines as much as possible. As Doody asserts, "if anybody has called a work a novel at any time, that is sufficient" (Doody 10) and further, "Romance and the novel are one" (Doody 15).

But as Eagleton admits, such definitions are so vague as to be functionally unusable. Contemporary histories and theories of the novel are thus content describing, rather than defining, the novel. These descriptions typically invoke realism, irony, individualism, empiricism, the middle-class, and a host of other possibilities. Ian Watt's development of "formal realism" in *The Rise of the Novel*, for example, focuses on a particularly novelistic deployment of Cartesian individualism in middle-class England as the driving force behind the development of the novel genre. In an oversimplification of Watt's argument, it can be said that the early British novel is defined as a work of prose fiction from the early eighteenth century that utilizes formal realism. Yet Watt's focus on formal realism is tied to his critical assertion that the formal realism found in the work of Defoe, Richardson, and Fielding constitutes the most important strain of legitimate novelistic discourse of the period, and thus his definition of the early British novel seems somewhat tautological in its assumptions.

But if Watt's definition of the novel is objectionably narrow in its insistence on formal realism and a clear break with prior prose fiction, definitions like those offered by Eagleton and Doody are so broad as to eliminate any real genre-specific boundaries on the novel. Though Doody correctly points out that contemporary historians of the novel too often rely on the critical framework and concerns of the late twentieth-century and more recent scholarship when defining and describing the early British novel, the practical intent of her argument seems to be to do away with any restrictions on the definition of the novel. Like Watt, Doody's definition of the novel is tied to her critical project – re-historicizing the novel as a persistent genre with its roots in the ancient near-east – and thus she is not at all concerned with assessing the significance of clearly identifiable changes in late seventeenth-century prose fiction that contributed to the development of what is now recognized as the British novel.

However, somewhere between the boundlessness of Doody's definition of the novel and Watt's insistence on tightly drawn boundaries lies a third approach to defining the genre. In *Before Novels*, J. Paul Hunter attempts to develop a culturally aware understanding of the way that prose fiction adopted the various characteristics that became associated with the Bakhtinian concept of "novelization" (Hunter 20–25) during the sixty years or so between 1680 and

1740, rather than insisting on a particular definition of the novel. Histories of the novel by Hunter, Nancy Armstrong, and Brean Hammond and Shaun Regan, for example, assume a more nuanced stance in which the novel is neither a specifically new genre, nor is it an ancient and persistent literary form. These histories and theories of the novel see the genre as species of prose fiction that began to accumulate and deploy a set of loosely recognizable characteristics during the late seventeenth and early eighteenth centuries which over time became recognized as typical features of novels. Hunter, for example, includes a list of ten characteristics of early novels which included contemporaneity, credibility and probability, familiarity, rejection of typical plots, tradition-free language, individualism and subjectivity, empathy and vicariousness, coherence and unity of design, inclusivity and digressiveness, and self-consciousness about innovation and novelty (Hunter 23-24) as foundational characteristics that later became associated with what is now recognized as the novel.

Hunter clearly understands that the boundaries of the early novel were flexible and porous, yet he asserts that a recognizable process of novelization within prose fiction seemed to accelerate throughout the shifting cultural milieu of the latter part of the seventeenth century and on into the eighteenth. Because his critical approach is so nuanced, Hunter pushes for a broad approach to historicizing the novel:

> [T]he emerging novel must be placed in a broader context of cultural history, insisting that popular thought and materials of everyday print—journalism, didactic materials with all kinds of religious and ideological directions, and private papers and histories—need to be seen as contributors to the social and intellectual world in which the novel emerged. (Hunter 5)

While it is commonplace to examine the various factors Hunter lists that contributed to the genre's development during the eighteenth century and its rise to prominence during the nineteenth, this call for a more complete awareness of how the novel developed within culture returns us to the question of the role of rhetorical theory in the development of the novel. When Hunter speaks of a broader cultural context, he encourages the exploration of the full range of intellectual and cultural influences that came to bear on the earliest novelistic discourse, and to truly consider the full range of influences Hunter speaks of, British rhetorical theory must be included in our attempts to historicize the development of the British novel.

But just as it is notoriously difficult to define the novel, it is equally difficult to describe the significance of rhetoric within the cultural context of eighteenth-century Britain. During the eighteenth century, rhetoric began to push beyond the strictures of classical rhetorical theory. The rise of empiricism in science and philosophy filtered into rhetorical theory and rhetoric began to take on a decidedly epistemological function. Scottish rhetoricians began to gravitate toward theories of cognition offered by Thomas Reid, David Hartley, and Joseph Priestley while incorporating the aesthetic theories of David Hume and Edmund Burke in their development of a rhetorical theory concerned with taste and judgement. This shift toward epistemology in rhetoric had a far-reaching impact, though that impact is difficult to trace. Training in rhetoric was part of the British educational system at every level, and rhetorical works were some of the most widely printed and distributed texts of the eighteenth century. Thomas P. Miller observes that rhetoricians were some of the first scholars to examine British literature with a truly critical lens because of the moral dimension of rhetorical theory. Miller asserts that the eighteenth-century rhetorical emphasis on taste and judgment, fused with the classical rhetoric's concern for promoting cultural values, resulted in the development of literary critical structures within rhetorical theory, intended to impart a holistic cultural sense of aesthetics to a rapidly expanding reading public (Miller 8).

Despite the pervasiveness and importance of rhetoric during the novel's early development, British rhetorical theory of the eighteenth and nineteenth centuries has largely been left out of the history of the novel. This is not to say that rhetorical concepts clearly present in the development of the novel have been ignored by contemporary literary historians. Instead, critics and scholars have often viewed rhetoric's function in the development of the novel within a narrow search for the application of specific rhetorical strategies at work within the early British novel. Perhaps the best-known example of this kind of scholarship is found in Wayne Booth's *The Rhetoric of Fiction*, in which Booth attempts to identify the various rhetorical strategies and devices deployed in early British novels. While this scholarship is valuable for its ability to show rhetorical theory at work within specific novels, this should not be the only approach to understanding the relationship between rhetoric and the British novel.

The startling range of intellectual interests that found expression in eighteenth-century rhetorical theory is too often overlooked or dismissed as "the commonplaces of the time" (Owen qtd. in Wu 24) and not truly relevant to any serious critical evaluation of the history of the novel. This is evident in literary histories of English studies: disciplinary historians such as Gerald Graff begin their histories of English studies with the formal inclusion of English language literature in the academy, giving only passing notice to the earlier inclusion of rhetoric and composition courses with endowed chairs throughout eighteenth-century Scottish universities. Miller asserts that this disregard for rhetoric's critical function has much to do with the development of English as an academic discipline:

> The appearance of professorships and textbooks [during the latter half of the eighteenth century] marks the formation of English as an object of established study in higher education, but histories of the discipline have been hesitant to accept eighteenth-century professors of rhetoric as the founders of college English because they did not establish literary discourse as a specialized area of study. (Miller 2)

Hayden White goes so far as to argue that the emergence of literature in the nineteenth century necessitated the suppression of rhetoric as an academic discipline, even though rhetoric prior to the nineteenth century served as a critical apparatus for the entire range of possible discourse: "prosaic and poetic; narrative and dissertative; factual, fictive, and mixed; communicative, expressive, and performative . . . were treated as instances [of speech as discourse], the relations among which were presumed to be identifiable" (White 21). But even if the relationship of eighteenth-century rhetoric to the development of literary criticism has been largely ignored by contemporary historians of English studies, the relevance of rhetoric to the study of literature was perfectly clear to many nineteenth-century critics, including David Masson, Henry Morley, and George Saintsbury.

For these reasons, eighteenth-century rhetorical theory is an important part of the history of the novel. Rhetoricians of the eighteenth century sought to revise and apply classical rhetorical theory to a broad cross-section of enlightenment concerns including taste, judgment, sentiment, cognition, epistemology, psychology, aesthetic theory, morality and ethics, and of course, literary criticism. Eighteenth-century rhetoricians, influenced by empiricist philosophical developments, pushed to move beyond the boundaries of the classical rhetorical model that had survived, largely intact, from the time of Quintilian; as a result, rhetorical theory became increasingly concerned with the reception of texts rather than their production. This move toward theories of reception pushed rhetoric toward an association with criticism and by the middle of the eighteenth century many rhetoricians saw almost no difference between rhetoric and criticism. This conflation of rhetoric with criticism continued into the nineteenth century, as criticism eventually subsumed rhetoric in the newly formed university English departments[1]. In its continuing shift away from production and toward reception, eighteenth-century revisions to rhetorical theory provided the framework for the critical structures that accompanied the development of the novel throughout the eighteenth and nineteenth centuries.

---

[1] Thomas P. Miller lucidly describes the transition of rhetoric to criticism within the academy in his 1997 study, *The Formation of College English*.

So while the relationship between rhetoric and the novel is certainly a real and under-developed strain in the history of the novel, the instability of each term – rhetoric and the novel – makes pursuing the relationship between the two devilishly difficult: if we refuse both overly-restrictive definitions like Watt's as well as vague non-definitions like those offered by Doody and Eagleton, how do we know what is or is not a novel? And if rhetoric was rapidly shifting toward criticism during the eighteenth century, why not simply discard the term "rhetoric" in favor of its nineteenth-century manifestation, criticism? Because this study attempts to develop a historically sensitive understanding of the interaction between the development of the British novel and simultaneous changes in rhetorical theory, I will not attempt to develop a single definition of the novel or of rhetoric. Instead, through referencing contemporary eighteenth- and nineteenth-century definitions and descriptions, I will show that both the novel and rhetoric were well-established though highly flexible concepts amidst the rapid changes taking place in novelistic discourse and rhetorical theory.

In the case of the novel, I will rely in part on definitions and descriptions developed by eighteenth and nineteenth century novelists and critics. Despite Watt's insistence that British novelists "did not even canonize the changed nature of their fiction by a change in nomenclature . . . until the end of the eighteenth century" (Watt 10), there are instances of novelists defining the nature of the novel prior to 1800. One of the earliest definitions of the British novel is found in William Congreve's *Incognita*. Published in 1692, the preface to *Incognita* contains a succinct and clearly delineated description of the novel in opposition to the romance: "Novels are of a more familiar nature; Come near us, and represent to us Intrigues in practice, delight us with Accidents and odd Events, but not such as are wholly unusual or unpresidented [sic], such which not being so distant from our Belief bring also the pleasure nearer us" (Congreve, preface to *Incognita*). Congreve's novel then proceeds to demonstrate this difference between the romance and the novel by re-conceptualizing the familiar romance conventions of chivalry, courtliness, and star-crossed lovers within a clearly novelistic framework.

Nearly a century later, in 1785, Clara Reeve gives a similar definition when she describes the novel in *The Progress of Romance:*

> The Novel is a picture of real life and manners, and of the times in which it is written. The Romance in lofty and elevated language, describes what never happened nor is likely to happen. – The Novel gives a familiar relation of such things, as pass every day before our eyes, such as may happen to our friend, or to ourselves; and the perfection of it, is to represent every scene, in so easy and natural a manner, and to make them appear so probable, as to deceive us into a persuasion (at least while we are reading) that all is real." (Reeve, preface to *The Progress of Romance* n.p).

It is worth noting that the concept of the novel seems to have remained relatively stable for most of the eighteenth century. Of course, Congreve and Reeve represent only two examples of explicit generic awareness of the novel; however, there are countless implicit examples of this same awareness delivered by authors throughout the eighteenth century who purposefully and pointedly include the term "novel" in the titles of their prose fiction.

The use of the term "novel" is further muddied, however, by other eighteenth-century designations for what we have come to recognize as the novel: two of the most problematic include "true history" and "new romance." Yet these terms represent an awareness shared by early novelists that their work was somehow distinct from previous conceptions of history or romance. The term that stuck to this emerging form of prose fiction – the novel – clearly indicates that these works were somehow different than prior literary forms. The fact that novelists like Congreve and Reeve were consciously drawing distinctions between their novels and other forms of prose fiction demonstrates an awareness of genre that should not be glossed over or forgotten simply because the genre terminology of the eighteenth-century was in flux. Such genre awareness – offered by some of the earliest novelists – pushes at both the highly restrictive and intentionally vague poles of novel definitions offered by twentieth- and twenty-first century scholars. My conception of the novel, then, will rest in part on the descriptions offered by those authors who, like Congreve and Reeve, were in the thick of writing and thinking about the earliest members of the novel species.

Rhetoric is somewhat less easy to pin down than the novel. Perhaps one of the best ways to understand the vast range of intellectual activity grouped under the heading of rhetoric during the eighteenth century is to borrow the heuristic developed by Douglas Ehninger which provides a useful overview of the strains of thought associated with British rhetorical theory during the eighteenth century. Ehninger argues that there were four major areas of emphasis in eighteenth-century British rhetorical thought: classical rhetoric, elocutionary rhetoric, psychological-epistemological rhetoric, and belle lettres rhetoric. These divisions do create some artificial boundaries which obscure overlap among the streams of thought, but his attention to the broad range of intellectual pursuits that found expression within rhetorical theory makes his work an excellent starting point for understanding the wide-reaching influence of eighteenth-century British rhetoric and its relationship to the novel.

Ehninger observes that eighteenth-century classical rhetoric – typified in John Ward's *A System of Oratory* (1759) – was a conservative approach to rhetoric that only minimally revised and refigured ancient rhetorical theory, particularly as conceived by Cicero and Quintilian. Elocutionary rhetoric focused almost exclusively on the classical rhetorical canon of delivery and developed elaborate

Definitions and Histories 19

and often cumbersome strategies for effective oratory. Neither of these strains of rhetoric proved influential into the nineteenth century: eighteenth-century classical rhetoric gradually devolved into basic mechanical systems of grammar and rote memorization, only faintly recalling its intellectually robust classical forbears, while elocutionary rhetoric developed a reputation as a bizarre outgrowth of rhetoric with little practical value.

Psychological-epistemological rhetoric and *belle lettres* rhetoric, however, each had a lasting and meaningful impact on rhetorical theory and practice, as well as advancing much of the intellectual basis for literary criticism during the nineteenth century. Psychological-epistemological rhetoric, typified by George Campbell's *Philosophy of Rhetoric*, sought to understand how and why rhetoric functioned. Psychological-epistemological rhetoric interacted with a broad range of intellectual thought, particularly the commonsense philosophy of Thomas Reid and Joseph Priestley, and brought theories of epistemology, cognition, and linguistics together with a rhetorical concern for the production and reception of effective written and oral texts. Campbell's work epitomizes a movement within eighteenth-century rhetorical theory to understand the relationship between language and cognition, emphasizing the importance of individual experience in making meaning.

Belle lettres rhetoric, perhaps best embodied in Hugh Blair's *Lectures on Rhetoric and Belles Lettres*, focused on taste and judgment and helped systematize and disseminate the aesthetic structures of intellectuals like Nicolas Boileau, Edmund Burke, and David Hume, as well as the cognitive theories of Thomas Reid, Joseph Priestley, and David Hartley. Importantly, Blair attempted to show how these aesthetic and epistemological concerns might be applied to both the production and reception of texts, including the novel. In Lecture XXXVII of *Lectures on Rhetoric and Belles Lettres*, Blair develops a brief history of "fictitious histories" beginning in ancient Rome, progressing through the "heroic romance" of medieval Europe and finally discussing the merits of the "Familiar Novel" (Blair 421–4). Blair focuses on the importance of taste and judgment in the reception of novels:

> [F]icticious histories might be employed for very useful purposes. They furnish one of the best channels for conveying instruction, for painting human life and manners, for showing the errors into which we are betrayed by our passions, for rendering virtue amiable and vice odious. The effect of well contrived stories... is stronger than any effect that can be produced by simple and naked instruction. (Blair 421)

Blair goes on to briefly evaluate some of what he considers to be the more admirable members of the novel species, discussing the virtues of *Gil Blas*, *Robinson Crusoe*, *Tom Jones*, and *Clarissa*. Blair's evaluations are closely tied to his belief in the virtuous nature of good art, and his deployment of belletristic rhetoric as a critical framework is significant. Blair is of course not the first or only person to develop such a justification for novel reading and writing. However, the wide distribution and contemporary praise for his *Lectures on Rhetoric and Belles Lettres* give some indication of his importance in the Romantic period, a concept which will be explored at length in Chapter 4.

Rhetoric, Criticism, and the Novel

To understand how eighteenth-century rhetorical theory affected nineteenth-century novel criticism, it is first necessary to understand that the emergence of the novel as a genre paralleled the development of a new, specifically British rhetoric. This dual development was no coincidence and was driven by the rapid growth of empiricism in philosophical and scientific thought. Empiricism, here understood broadly as a wide range of eighteenth-century thought that emphasized observable experience, naturally contributed to the development of the novel as a genre largely dependent on the closely observed experiences of its characters. And while empiricist thought provided much of the impetus behind the development of the novel as a distinct genre, it simultaneously exerted a great deal of influence on eighteenth-century rhetorical theory, which increasingly turned toward the individual as the interpreter of experience and creator of meaning. In describing the influence of "New Rhetoricians" such as Adam Smith, George Campbell, Hugh Blair, Joseph Priestley, and James Beattie on British Romanticism, James Engell observes that though this new rhetoric drew on classical rhetorical theory, it "subordinate[d] formal divisions, long lists of terms, and rote strategies in favor of a robust psychological approach, natural style, and a firm linguistic . . . foundation" (Engell 218). Further, this new Rhetoric was intended "as . . . a complete system of criticism and a guide to improving style and taste" (Engell 218). This emphasis on style, taste, and judgment created a new breed of rhetoric concerned far more with the reception, rather than the production, of texts.

It was in the work of Scottish rhetoricians in the second half of the eighteenth century that systems of rhetoric truly became systems of criticism. Neil Rhodes cites Robert Watson's rhetoric lecture series at St. Andrews University, first delivered in 1758, as the first instance of rhetoric and criticism becoming fully interchangeable terms. In his lectures, Watson conflates rhetoric with criticism:

> By the Rules of Rhetorick are meant Nothing else, but Observations concerning the Particulars which render Discourse excellent & usefull. It is not proposed to deliver them in the Form of Rules, but in the form of general Criticisms illustrated by Examples from Authors. To what follows then you may give the Name of Rhetorick, or Criticism if you please; if they deserve the one they will deserve the other also. (qtd. in Rhodes 29)

Ehninger has observed that this shift came about because belletrism pushed rhetoric to become "almost exclusively a speculative science concerned with judging" and removed virtually all former traces of rhetoric's traditional generative function (Ehninger 306).

This connection between rhetoric and criticism is clearly evident in Hugh Blair's widely read *Lectures on Rhetoric and Belles Lettres*. While Adam Smith's earlier lectures of the same name focused on style and the development of taste, Blair's lecture series expanded and enlarged Smith's ideas into a more complete system of criticism that focused on the relationship of taste, judgment, and the sublime. In their introduction to Blair's *Lectures*, Linda Ferreira-Buckley and S. Michael Halloran emphasize this shift, observing that Blair's lectures responded to the reading public's desire to develop a cohesive national sense of taste and judgment; accordingly, Blair's rhetoric "shifted emphasis from a generative to an analytic art" (Ferreira-Buckley and Halloran xv). Lecture III of Blair's *Lectures on Rhetoric and Belles Lettres* focuses on criticism and taste and begins with a succinct definition of criticism: "[t]rue Criticism is the application of Taste and of good sense to the several fine arts" (Blair 121). Furthermore, Blair earlier states that "[c]riticism is an art founded wholly on experience" (Blair 21), demonstrating the indebtedness of belletristic rhetoric to empiricist philosophy. Blair understood taste to be an inborn faculty common to everyone; however, taste was not present in the same proportion or acuteness in everyone. This natural faculty could also be expanded and cultivated through contact with works of art, literature, and music that were broadly acknowledged to be works of genius. These ideas were to have great currency as literary criticism developed during the nineteenth century.

Blair also conceived rhetoric as serving a unique civic function. The moralistic function of classical rhetoric, perhaps best exemplified in Quintilian's insistence on the prerequisite virtue of a true rhetor, placed the civic value of rhetoric in its ability to help a good man learn to speak well in public. George A. Kennedy observes that Blair regarded Quintilian's work as "the authoritative statement of classical rhetoric" (Kennedy 118). Yet Blair and *belles lettres* turned this function of rhetoric inward. Instead of Quintilian's good man speaking well, Blair asserts that his lectures might offer students the prospect of "acquir[ing] principles which will enable them to judge for themselves" (Blair 5) concerning literature and art without the civic obligation of delivering such judgments to the public at large. Blair's *Lectures* certainly did not neglect oratory, and Blair readily subscribed to much of Quintilian's thought on the civic function of oratory. But the *Lectures* have a decidedly individualistic emphasis on the power of great art to develop the twin faculties of taste and judgment, and Blair devotes much more of the *Lectures* to these concerns than he does to oratory.

Still, the question of taste and judgment was also a question of public virtue for Blair, and one of the purposes of his lecture series was to equip the public with the knowledge necessary to form accurate judgments on an individual level, thereby broadly shaping a cohesive societal conception of taste (Blair 22). The intertwined relationship of the aesthetic and moral dimensions of art so important in the belletristic conception of taste and judgment continued to reverberate in the novel criticism of the nineteenth century. Concerns over the moral function of literature – and specifically the novel – can be widely seen throughout nineteenth century criticism, including, to varying degrees, in the work of critics like Harriet Martineau, George Eliot, Dinah Craik Mulock, Margaret Oliphant, and Henry James. These intertwined concerns are cited by Marthe Robert as one of the defining characteristics of the genre (Robert 63); further, the tension between the aesthetic and ethical nature of literature is a central concern within the revisions to rhetorical theory which took place during the eighteenth century.

And while Blair's is hardly the only eighteenth-century voice arguing for the moral influence of the arts, the impact of Blair's lectures is hard to overestimate: Thomas P. Miller cites the *Lectures* as going through one hundred ten editions after the first printing in 1783 (Miller 2), and Blair's lectures at Edinburgh proved so successful that in 1762 Blair was appointed as the university's first Regius Professor of Rhetoric and Belles Lettres, a post later re-named the Regius Professor of Literature and Belles Lettres and filled by well-known Victorian critics David Masson and George Saintsbury (Golden and Corbett 24). Saintsbury later praised Blair for "'accepting to the full the important truth that 'Rhetoric' in modern times really means 'Criticism'" (Saintsbury 196).

Despite these important connections between nineteenth-century critics like Masson and Saintsbury and their eighteenth-century antecedents in rhetoric, the impact of rhetoric in the development of nineteenth-century systems of criticism has been largely overlooked. As Lois Agnew observes, the contributions of rhetoric to criticism are often elided and further, "there has been a vague assumption that during the nineteenth century rhetoric . . . abruptly vanished in Britain and was spontaneously replaced by the study of literature" (Agnew 21). This study is concerned with the inverse of Agnew's observation: refuting the assumption that during the nineteenth century, literary criticism simply appeared, fully formed. The truth is just the opposite: the belletristic rhetoric of Hugh Blair, Lord Kames, George Campbell, Joseph Priestley, and Adam Smith contributed to the intellectual development of many Romantic and Victorian critics: William Hazlitt studied under Joseph Priestley (Miller 57); Thomas De Quincey's *Essays on Rhetoric* maintain sharp distinctions between eloquence and rhetoric, emphasize style, and make numerous allusions to belletristic principles (Burwick xxviii); and Masson was trained at the University of Edinburgh where Hugh Blair delivered his highly successful lectures on belles lettres and where in 1865 Masson began his thirty-year tenure as Professor of Rhetoric and English Literature (Eigner and Worth 148).

Thus, re-integrating eighteenth-century British rhetoric into the history of the novel is important for several reasons. Perhaps most important is the lack of scholarship studying the development of British rhetorical theory and the novel within a shared cultural discourse. Treatments of the novel and rhetoric typically focus on rhetorical devices: Wayne Booth's *The Rhetoric of Fiction* has already been mentioned, but other scholarship of this type includes Glen McClish's 1987 dissertation, *Rhetoric and the Rise of the Novel*. A brief glance at scholarly articles concerning rhetoric and the novel produces results that focus on the application of rhetorical devices in fiction and rarely – if ever – consider rhetoric outside this narrow definition. There are, of course, exceptions. As previously mentioned, James Engell argues that Scottish rhetoricians of the late eighteenth century are vastly underappreciated (Engell 217). Yet there are relatively few studies which consider the impact of these rhetoricians on the development of novel criticism during the nineteenth century.

Part of the problem is semantic: by the middle of the nineteenth century, the term rhetoric no longer encompassed a robust range of intellectual pursuits; instead, rhetoric began to formally break away from criticism. Hayden White observes that the separation of belles lettres from traditional rhetorical discourse was roughly contemporary with the elevation of literature to a special aesthetic status within Victorian culture (White 22–23). Patricia Bizzell and Bruce Herzberg echo White's position, arguing that rhetoric and criticism diverged during the nineteenth century because of the increasing departmentalization of the academy, the rapid expansion of composition courses, and the view, expressed by Coleridge and others, that poetry and rhetoric were entirely separate disciplines (Bizzell and Herzberg 994). Nevertheless, many nineteenth-century critics, including Thomas De Quincey, William Hazlitt, David Masson, Henry Morley, Walter Pater, and George Saintsbury all acknowledged the contributions of rhetoric to criticism. The civic function of rhetoric and the belletristic attempts to develop a cohesive national aesthetic through rhetorical training reverberates throughout much of the periodical criticism of the novel throughout the nineteenth century and reflects a clear indebtedness of the critical contributions of eighteenth-century rhetoric in the development of nineteenth-century criticism. Thus, the shifting terminology of the nineteenth century should not conceal the eighteenth-century emergence of a cultural discourse clearly shared by rhetoricians, novelists, and the reading public.

Rhetoric's reintegration into the story of the novel, then, is a matter of recovering the discourse shared by rhetoric and the novel. Because rhetoric, in its various permutations, was a central component in British education and culture throughout the novel's emergence during the eighteenth century and during its rise to prominence in the nineteenth century, reassessing the history of the novel in relation to British rhetorical theory of the same era provides a more complete understanding of the novel's development within Hunter's "broader context of cultural history" (Hunter 5). I am not attempting to write an alternate history of the novel and my approach is not specifically in opposition to any other histories of the genre. Instead, this study is intended to highlight the cultural relevance of examining the novel's emergence within the context of rhetorical theory, especially regarding the intersection of rhetoric with the moral and artistic functions of the novel within novel criticism of the late eighteenth and early nineteenth centuries. Thus, this history is not intended to replace other conceptions of the novel's development; instead, providing an additional layer of context to the history of the novel should enhance other histories of the genre. I return to Marthe Robert's identification of the novel as a genre caught up in "the inextricable combination of ethics and aesthetics" (Robert 63). This relationship is at the heart of this project, and I hope to offer some answers concerning how the novel, through its relationship to belletristic rhetoric, became the literary location where British writers and readers of the eighteenth and nineteenth centuries attempted to reconcile the tension between artistic function and moral purpose.

Chapter 3

French *Belles Lettres* and the Early British Novel: William Congreve's *Incognita*

> *Novels are of a more familiar Nature; Come near us, and represent to us Intrigues in practice, delight us with Accidents and odd Events, but not such as are wholly unusual or unpresidented . . . Romances give more of Wonder, Novels more Delight.*
>
> William Congreve, Preface to Incognita

The intertwined history of British novels, rhetoric, and criticism begins where most histories of the British novel begin, in the latter part of the seventeenth century amidst the profusion of imaginative prose fiction that developed in the late Restoration. The imaginative fiction of this time was transitional: it was often no longer recognizable as prose romance, yet it was still not quite recognizable as the early British novel of the eighteenth century. Instead, the work of Delarivier Manley, Eliza Haywood, Aphra Behn, and William Congreve demonstrates the novel as a genre in progress. Novelization, in the now-familiar formulation developed in Mikhail Bakhtin's *Dialogic Imagination*, refers to Bakhtin's assertion that the novel is a yet-unfinished genre. In opposition to other "completed" literary genres – and especially the epic – Bakhtin argues that "the novel is the sole genre that continues to develop, that is as yet uncompleted" (Bakhtin 3). Bakhtin describes the process of novelization as one in which literary works of all genres participate:

> They become more free and flexible, their language renews itself by incorporating extraliterary heteroglossia and the 'novelistic' layers of literary language, they become dialogized, permeated with laughter, irony, humor, elements of self-parody and finally – this is the most important thing – the novel inserts into these other genres an indeterminacy, a certain semantic openendedness, a living contact with unfinished, still-evolving contemporary reality. (Bakhtin 7)

Though Bakhtin's understanding of the novel focuses primarily on the linguistic and semantic effects of novelization, J. Paul Hunter recognizes Bakhtin's work as instrumental in releasing novel criticism from "thinking about novels in purely formal terms" (Hunter 361). Hunter uses the Bakhtinian concept of novelization to develop a set of novelistic characteristics that were increasingly manifested in the prose fiction of the late seventeenth century. In *Making the Novel*, Brean Hammond and Shaun Regan describe novelization as "a cultural process . . . making for the mingling and mixing of different literary modes within and between all the major genres" (Hammond and Regan 21). Thus, novelization is the process whereby prose fiction began accreting and deploying characteristics that distinguish the novel from its forebears in romance and epic. Such a view of the novel's origins insists that the novel be viewed as a cultural phenomenon in dialogue with a broad range of cultural, social, and historical influences.

Novelization thus refigures the genre's emergence in terms of competing ideologies and discourses (25) that are in constant contact or conflict with one another. These ideological shifts are familiar within the history of the novel: the emergence of empiricist thought in fields beyond science, the rapid expansion of the middle class, the growth of dissenting denominations and other familiar topoi are still part of the historical narrative of the novel, yet their effects, when viewed through the lens of novelization, do not lead to the emergence of a clearly identifiable set of formal novel characteristics. Instead, the novel becomes the literary location where these ideological concerns coalesce and interact with one another. The novel in this sense becomes the literary site of cultural discourse or discourses: as Hammond and Regan assert, "[the novel] is characterized more by certain kinds of discourses with particular ideological agendas, than it is by specific formal features associated with genre" (25). I argue that the genre-ness of the novel is found – at least in part – in its ability to respond and adapt to specific kinds of ideological discourse, particularly concerning virtue.

Novelization and *Letteraturizzazione*

It is worth comparing the concept of novelization to changes in rhetorical theory of roughly the same period. Like its counterpart in prose fiction, rhetoric of the late Restoration and early eighteenth century was in flux as rhetoricians confronted the implications of empiricist developments in science and philosophy. The Enlightenment notion that individual cognition grounded individual existence fostered major changes in cognitive theory. As the individual's experience became the arbiter of the individual's understanding of the natural world, those experiences took on a magnified sense of importance. In broad terms, truth was no longer approached only through a classical understanding of general, universal principles. Classicism's emphasis on an idealized conception of artistic expression implicitly rejected any focus on the individual. As Walter Jackson Bate observes, "classicism [was] not opposed only to the naturalistic but to any other conception of art which can be designated as personal or local" (Bate 11). Bate goes on to claim that classicism is inherently opposed to the empiricist emphasis on the individual because "[c]lassicism does not subscribe... to the belief that man's feelings and responses are themselves inherently good" (12). However, as classicism gave way to empiricist assumptions about individual cognition and perception, truth was increasingly understood to be located in an examination of the particular and individual, through experience and the interpretation of experience. The emphasis on the individual that resulted in the reevaluation of generic categories heavily influenced seventeenth and eighteenth-century theories of linguistics and semiotics.

Of course, in the seventeenth-century linguistics and semiotics were the purview of rhetoric, a discipline with an incredibly broad field of inquiry. Hayden White observes that "pre-nineteenth-century rhetorics recognized the figurative and tropical nature of all linguistic conventions and made of this recognition the basis of a general theory of speech as discourse" (White 21). George Kennedy argues that the breadth of inquiry associated with rhetoric gives rise to a cyclical process known as *letteraturizzazione*, a process that mirrors many of the same concerns as Bakhtin's novelization. Kennedy defines *letteraturizzazione* as "the tendency of rhetoric to shift focus from persuasion to narration, from civic to personal contexts, and from speech to literature" (3); he later describes it as "the 'literaturization' of rhetoric" (129). While Bakhtin argues that literature is susceptible to cycles of novelization in which all genres become increasingly concerned with dialogue and linguistic instability, *letteraturizzazione* suggests that rhetorical theory is subject to similar shifts that emphasize textuality over orality, narrative rather than persuasion, and the individual instead of the collective. Novelization and *letteraturizzazione* thus both point toward the development of the novel at the end of the seventeenth century, as prose fiction became increasingly dialogic, turning toward Bakhtinian elements of "laughter, irony, humor, elements of self-parody and ... semantic openendedness" (Bakhtin 7) while invoking *letteraturizzazione*'s rhetorical shift toward narration, personal context, and literariness.

Some of the basis for the accelerated processes of novelization and *letteraturizzazione* at the end of the seventeenth century can be located within the linguistic instability caused by the extension of empiricist principles into questions of language and semiotics. These questions are addressed by John Locke in his *Inquiry Concerning Human Understanding*. Though Locke was not a rhetorician, James Engell describes Locke as "a seminal figure" in the revision of rhetoric throughout the eighteenth century because of the impact of his cognitional theory. Locke's *Essay Concerning Human Understanding*, Engell argues, is a vital component in understanding new rhetoric's emphasis on the ways a hearer or reader responds to and receives discourse. Locke's empiricist concerns over the semiotic instability of language provided a starting point for rhetoricians to begin re-conceiving the purpose and function of discourse

(Engell 225). Additionally, James Sambrook asserts that Locke's theories concerning perception are central to understanding eighteenth-century aesthetic theory (Sambrook 101). Thus, Lockean theories of linguistics and semiotics are important to this study for two reasons.

First, Locke's concern about the subjectivity inherent in understanding and communicating complex concepts through language affords the opportunity to explore the slippery genre terminology – such as "true history" and "new romance" – that surrounds some of the earliest species of the novel. A brief examination of Locke thus provides vital context for understanding that though "novel" was hardly the consensus term for the new wave of prose fiction that emerged at the beginning of the eighteenth century, the concepts associated with the idea of what came to be known as the novel were already well established.

Second, and more importantly, an examination of Locke's efforts to promote a semiotic structure that would provide stability for the apprehension of complex concepts and ideas is a clear precursor to efforts within eighteenth-century rhetorical theory to create a cohesive cultural standard of taste and judgment. As Barbara Warnick argues in *The Sixth Canon*, the belletrists of the seventeenth and eighteenth centuries were heavily influenced by the empiricist understanding of sense perception and memory, and this influence formed the basis for the belletristic notion that "the aesthetic appeal of a discourse was essential to its rhetorical effect" (Warnick 6). Walter Jackson Bate observes that the effect of British empirical thought – with Locke as the standard bearer – spread broadly throughout British aesthetic theory of the eighteenth century. Importantly for any attempt to understand the history of the novel in relation to rhetorical theory, Bate asserts that these empirical tendencies in eighteenth-century rhetoric and aesthetic theory were grounded in ideas that have since become central tenets in describing the early British novel:

> [S]uch truth as can be known is to be found primarily in or through the particular, and that this truth is to be realized, appreciated, and declared in art by the response to that particular of some faculty or capacity in man which is imaginative and often emotional rather than 'rational,' and which therefore inclines to be somewhat individualistic and subjective in its working. (Bate 94)

Thus, Locke's concern with language and cognition strikes at the heart of the development of the early novel and helps clarify some of the conceptual motivation for the eighteenth-century revision of rhetoric's generative function into a focus on reception.

Locke and "the Imperfection of Words"

Locke's concerns with linguistic and semiotic instability are central in *An Essay Concerning Human Understanding*. Here, Locke confronts the problem of extending empiricist principles into the most basic functions of language. Through an examination of the application of empiricist principles to linguistic and semiotic questions, Locke articulates anxieties about language and cognition that would reverberate throughout the eighteenth century. His primary concern is with the effect of empiricist philosophy on semiotics. Locke confronts what he deems "the Imperfection of Words" resulting from individual experience becoming the central component in the creation and apprehension of meaning. Language, Locke argues, is ill-suited to the task of signifying meaning to individuals who, because of the differences in their specific experiences, may not always agree on the meaning of words. Though Locke admits that when we are developing our own, personal set of signifiers, any words will serve to "[record] our own thoughts for the help of our own memories" (817; bk. III, ch. IX), he voices concern over the ability of words to communicate meaning beyond our own thoughts. Locke maintains that though "the chief end of language in communication is to be understood," words are a poor tool for communication (817; bk. III, ch. IX). This is because the empiricist emphasis on individual experience injects a level of subjectivity into language that destabilizes notions of what words signify. Locke's primary concern lies in signifying complex ideas which have "no standards in nature" (818; bk III, ch. IX). Furthermore,

> They [complex ideas] are assemblages of ideas put together at the pleasure of the mind, pursuing its own ends of discourse, and suited to its own notions; whereby it designs not to copy anything really existing, but to denominate and rank things as they come to agree with those archetypes or forms it has made. (818; bk. III, ch. IX)

Thus, Locke argues that language, as a set of concrete, universally agreed upon signifiers, struggles to function efficiently in a highly subjective empiricist worldview.

Locke explains at some length that even words which seem fixed in their definitions are prone to misunderstanding and multiple complex meanings. As an example, Locke relates his experience discussing the effect of liquor on the nerves with a group of physicians. The doctors offered various arguments, but the discussion made little headway. The conversation could only make progress when Locke put forward the question of defining liquor and the physicians "found that the signification of that word was not so settled or certain as they had all imagined . . . This made them perceive that the main of their dispute was about the signification of that term" (822; bk. III, ch. IX). Furthermore, some words present difficulty because of the multiple meanings that can be intended by a single term. Locke's example is "gold," a term that he claims is deceptively simple. Gold seems to be a fixed signifier, but Locke observes that gold can refer to color or chemical properties or currency or jewelry. The conclusion is that "words have very uncertain significations" (823; bk. III, ch. IX), and thus we must be cautious when deploying language, especially concerning complex concepts like honor, faith, and grace because these words signify complex concepts that have no fixed examples in nature. In the end, disputes about the exact meaning of these complex signifiers become nothing more than "contests . . . about the meaning of a sound" (819; bk. III, ch. IX).

While Locke allows that common usage can and frequently does alleviate some of these issues, the problem of language and meaning is most apparent in the use of "moral words" (818; bk. III, ch. IX). The shifting meaning of words that describe complex concepts forces us, in Locke's words, to practice "moderation in imposing our own sense of old authors" (824; bk. III, ch. IX). Here, Locke makes an argument for understanding language within its cultural context, asserting that the ancients should be examined with great care because changes in language, custom, and culture that occur across time necessarily affect our understanding, creating a circumstance in which exact meaning cannot be agreed upon "without a constant defining the terms" (824; bk. III, ch. IX).

The solution Locke offers to the semiotic and linguistic instability caused by the extension of empiricist principles into language is essentially a revision of rhetoric that focuses on clarity and order in discourse, eliminating "eloquence" in favor of perspicuity and propriety (827; bk. III, ch. X). Clarity and order – in rhetorical terms, perspicuity and propriety – were concepts at the center of the revisioning of rhetoric throughout the eighteenth century, and thus Locke's concerns, voiced in 1690[1], about the implications of a semiotic structure that had been reinterpreted through an empiricist, individualist worldview provides a starting point for understanding some of the ways in which empiricism affected not only the novel, but also led to large-scale revisions of rhetorical theory. Locke's assertion that complex signifiers present the most difficulty in developing a shared understanding of language sheds light on the quicksilver nature of the early British novel and the rapid shifts in rhetorical theory of roughly the same period. Thus, the examination of Locke also helps us resolve one of the most persistent difficulties in drawing out the connecting lines between the early British novel, eighteenth-century rhetoric, and nineteenth-century novel criticism: the problem of definition.

---

[1] It is worth noting that Locke's *Essay Concerning Human Understanding* was published in the thick of some of the earliest English-language novel publications, two years after Aphra Behn's *Oroonoko* and two years before William Congreve's *Incognita*.

With Locke's skeptical account regarding the operation of language as a guide, examining the novel in light of rhetorical theory invites an investigation of a shared range of concerns within an energetic discourse focused on resolving what Marthe Robert describes as the central tension of the early novel found in "the inextricable combination of ethics and aesthetics" (Robert 63). Robert is only thinking of the novel, but eighteenth-century rhetoric – and later, nineteenth-century criticism – continually confronted this problem. This shared discourse is perhaps best understood by first looking at two important critical efforts – Marthe Robert's aforementioned *Origins of the Novel* and Michael McKeon's *The Origins of the English Novel* – that identify within the early novel a discourse concerned with virtue and aesthetics.

As briefly mentioned in the previous chapter, identifying the earliest members of the novel species is a slippery task because the terminology used to describe the novel was still in flux: the early prose fiction that we now often categorize as "the novel" was referred to by a wide range of terms, with novel, new romance, and true history as perhaps the most persistent. As critics and scholars of the novel have long observed, the problem of defining the novel is plagued by the novel's endless flexibility: the novel is not a genre that can be defined by length or content or format. Aphra Behn's *Oroonoko* is relatively short, while Richardson's *Clarissa* is almost unbelievably long, with texts of every length falling somewhere in between. Clearly length is not the defining factor. Content does not seem to provide a better set of criteria for identifying the novel, though early novels are often concerned with ordinary people and their interaction with the world. Form is no use either. The novel appears in any number of guises and shows itself to be a remarkably flexible genre: the early British novel can appear to us as travelogue or confession, as letters and journal entries or memoir, as fabliaux or parody or satire or any number of other possibilities.

Robert argues that this infinite flexibility lies at the heart of the novel's character, asserting that "the novel's power resides precisely in its total freedom" (Robert 60) and goes on to her central claim that the novel is a genre "torn between innumerable external compulsions and swayed by the inextricable combination of ethics and aesthetics" (Robert 63). Robert's observation about the opposition of ethics and aesthetics within the development of the early novel strikes close to the heart of the problem in reassessing the novel in relationship to the rhetorical tradition. If the early novel was, as Robert claims, torn between the opposing poles of ethical and aesthetic purposes, then rhetorical theory of the same time could be seen as increasingly concerned with the reconciliation of ethics and aesthetics.

A useful way to view Robert's opposition of ethics and aesthetics as it developed during the eighteenth century is to contextualize it within the influence of empiricism on eighteenth-century thought. The influence of empiricism on the earliest strains of the British novel has become a well-established trope in histories of the genre. Ian Watt, for example, observes that there was a "growing tendency for the individual experience to replace collective tradition as the ultimate arbiter of reality" (Watt 14) beginning at least in the Renaissance, if not farther back. While the empiricist influence on the early British novel has been developed by a wide range of scholars, Michael McKeon's account of empiricism's effect on the culture in which the early novel emerged is worth examining here. In *The Origins of the English Novel*, McKeon argues that empiricism affected the development of the novel in two ways.

First, the empiricist emphasis on individual experience as the starting point for the creation of knowledge and meaning resulted in the de-stabilization of generic categories. On one level, as Locke argues, the emphasis on individual experience in the creation of knowledge destabilized the basic foundations of language; as these linguistic and cognitive concerns were extended throughout the Enlightenment, prior genre categories like romance and history were increasingly viewed through a lens of individual experience, calling into question the attending suppositions about the nature of truth and knowledge. Traditional literary transmitters of cultural knowledge – romance, history, epic, and poetry – came under close scrutiny during the Enlightenment as the individual became increasingly important as the arbiter of knowledge (McKeon, The *Origins of the English Novel* 25–52).

Second, the move toward the individual as arbiter of knowledge forced a re-assessment of ethical and moral codes, a process that caused the destabilization of social categories. McKeon argues that an "aristocratic ideology," which located virtue within the individual's birth and breeding, was reassessed under the pressure of a developing middle class that had no access to the inherited virtue of the landed aristocracy (McKeon, *The Origin of the English Novel* 131–133). McKeon asserts that the novel emerged under these circumstances as "a new literary fiction designed to engage the social and ethical problems the established literary fictions could no longer mediate" (McKeon, *The Origin of the English Novel* 133). These "Questions of Truth" and "Questions of Virtue" help us untangle the web surrounding the influence of empiricism on the early novel; additionally, McKeon's focus on truth and virtue allows us to begin evaluating how the same influences that fostered the development of the early British novel began to push rhetoric toward a close association with criticism.

This is because McKeon's heuristic, centered on truth and virtue, is essentially rhetorical: these twin concerns have been at the heart of rhetorical theory throughout the history of the discipline. Some of the earliest controversies surrounding the purpose and function of rhetoric have revolved around rhetoric's approach to truth and its attention to virtue. The history of rhetoric, in fact, begins with questions about truth and virtue in the development of competing strains of rhetoric in ancient Greece. George A. Kennedy[2] describes three approaches to rhetoric in the ancient tradition: technical rhetoric, sophistic rhetoric, and philosophical rhetoric. Technical rhetoric is described by Kennedy as "pragmatic; it shows how to present a subject efficiently and effectively" yet does not take into consideration the moral character of the rhetor or his arguments (Kennedy 14). The other two strains of ancient rhetoric, however, are deeply involved in questions of truth and virtue.

The first of these, sophistic rhetoric, was founded in part on Empedocles' assumption that because human knowledge is based on sense perceptions, it is necessarily flawed. To the sophists[3], the subjective nature of human knowledge seemed to render the apprehension of ultimate truth nearly impossible. Working from this epistemological underpinning, the sophists attempted to discover what was most probable – rather than what was ultimately true – through the application of logic in the disputation of opposing points of view (Bizzell and Herzburg 22). The sophists did not deny the existence of ultimate truth; rather, they asserted that because ultimate truth is inaccessible to the human mind, the exercise of rhetoric is best applied to what is probable. The *ethos* of the speaker thus looms large in the sophistic tradition: the virtue of the rhetor was important because, according to Kennedy, sophistic rhetoric "emphasizes the speaker rather than the speech or audience and is responsible for the image of the ideal orator leading society to noble fulfillment of national ideals" (Kennedy 14).

This image of a persuasive public figure, exerting influence on the masses by focusing on what was probable rather than what was true led to attacks on sophistic rhetoric by later rhetoricians and philosophers. In the *Gorgias* and the *Phaedrus*, for example, Plato attempts to develop an understanding of true and false rhetoric. Plato attacks the sophists for failing to focus on ultimate truth and argues that it is a misapplication of rhetoric to "simply entertain and manipulate"[4] (Bizzell and Herzberg 29). Instead, Plato argues, rhetoric should be used to discover and convey truth. In the *Phaedrus*, Plato insists that a true rhetor should focus on truth and morality, and asserts that no matter how

---

[2] Kennedy's work on the history of rhetoric has certainly been challenged and reassessed in recent years; nevertheless, his lucid, cogent description of the major movements within the discipline provides an excellent entry into an examination of the history of rhetoric.

[3] Though much recent scholarship suggests that the sophistic tradition hardly represents a single, monolithic point of view, I am using the term to encapsulate a broad range of ancient rhetorical thought in opposition to the Platonic conception of rhetoric.

[4] Charges of this sort, of course, are frequently leveled at the novel throughout the eighteenth and nineteenth centuries.

persuasive a speaker might be, the moral component of their speech and their character is of the highest importance: "[I]gnorance of right and wrong and good and bad is in truth inevitably a disgrace, even if the whole mob applaud it" (Plato, *Phaedrus* 167). From the beginning, then, rhetoric has concerned itself with contested approaches to and conceptualizations of truth and virtue.

As McKeon's heuristic highlights, the concerns with truth and virtue that manifested in the emerging novel were clearly important to rhetorical theory relationship of the same time; thus, because rhetorical theory had long been concerned with the relationship between truth and virtue, McKeon's heuristic allows us to begin examining a discourse, concerned with truth and virtue, which appeared within both the developing novel and within the revisions to rhetoric that took place during the eighteenth century. The internal struggle between ethics and aesthetics that Robert identifies as one of the key characteristics of the early novel is present in McKeon's "Questions of Truth" and "Questions of Virtue." The critical practice of examining the tension between the aesthetic and ethical function of the newly emergent British novel can be seen, then, as essentially rhetorical in nature.

But while demonstrating the relationship of rhetoric to the discourse and meta-discourse of the British novel requires an examination of beginnings, almost immediately a difficulty arises: the timelines of rhetorical revisions and the emergence of the British novel do not line up precisely. The two develop side by side and share many of the same core concerns, yet that development occurs in fits and starts: the novel charges ahead and by the middle of the eighteenth-century, a set of "novelistic" characteristics had emerged (Hunter 23–25). British rhetorical theory, by contrast, clung to its classical roots until closer to the century's mid-point, when Scottish intellectuals such as Robert Watson, Adam Smith, and Lord Kames began formally revising rhetoric through university lectures and critical essays, accelerating the transition of rhetoric from a generative to an analytical discipline.

The task of identifying the relationship between rhetoric and novelistic discourse becomes much clearer toward the end of the eighteenth century; however, as the eighteenth century begins this relationship is decidedly muddy. Yet an examination of early British novelistic fiction and roughly contemporary rhetorical theory provides an important basis for understanding the long-term relationship among the British novel, novel criticism, and rhetoric. Here, McKeon's "Questions of Truth" and "Questions of Virtue" return us to Locke's struggle with Empiricism and semiotics. Inherent in McKeon's heuristic is an eighteenth-century cultural acknowledgement, whether tacit or overt, of a shift in the conception of truth and virtue. These are precisely the kinds of concepts Locke has in mind as he describes the "imperfection of words" caused by the application of Empiricist principles of subjectivity to language. Locke's concerns about the shortcomings of language are central to McKeon's understanding of "Questions of Truth" and invite us to look to one of the earliest intersections of shifting rhetorical theory and novelistic discourse within William Congreve's 1692 proto-novel, *Incognita; or, Love and Duty Reconcil'd*.

French *Belles Lettres* in Congreve's *Incognita*

I make no claims concerning *Incognita* as the first British novel, but my method throughout this study will be to look for specific, identifiable instances where rhetorical theory and the novel intersect in both the novel itself and the discourse surrounding the novel. In this regard, *Incognita* is a perfect place to begin. If we look to other scholars, we find Ian Watt considers Betteredge's old friend *Robinson Crusoe* the first novel in English. Watt's identification of Defoe's novel as first is, of course, predicated on Watt's critical conception of formal realism and there is a valid argument to be made for the centrality of a new kind of realism in the prose fiction which emerged during the late seventeenth century and coalesced in the work of Defoe and Richardson, though Watt struggles to shoehorn his realism criteria onto Fielding's novels. In recent years, Aphra Behn's *Oroonoko* has been brought to the forefront of discussions about the earliest members of the genre in English and Behn's novel certainly predates *Robinson Crusoe* by almost three decades. *Oroonoko* possesses several characteristics which might be described, to use J. Paul Hunter's terminology, as novelistic. Behn, along with contemporaries such as Delarivier Manley and Eliza Haywood, wrote fiction that paid close attention to their characters' subjectivity, focusing on their interior lives and thoughts, presenting a realistic portrayal of psychological depth that was a marked departure from prior traditions, particularly prose romance.

In Congreve's *Incognita*, though, prose fiction is in a transitional state. *Incognita* is clearly indebted to the Restoration and romance tradition for its aristocratic characters and Italian setting. Samuel Johnson relates that contemporary criticism of *Incognita* was complimentary, though Johnson dismisses Congreve's novel, sniffing that he "would rather praise it than read it" (Johnson, *Lives* 201). The comic elements are familiar: there are star-crossed lovers, mistaken identities, secret assignations, and the looming presence of powerful parents exerting their will on younger generations. The basic outlines of the plot are typical of the romance tradition and Restoration comedy: two young aristocrats (Aurelian and Hippolito) are attempting to pass through Florence in disguise to avoid detection by Aurelian's father, who has arranged what Aurelian imagines can only be a distasteful marriage. At a ball in Florence, the two young men meet two young women. Hippolito is smitten with Leonora; Aurelian with Juliana who, unbeknownst to him, is the woman intended for him by his father. For reasons of pressing concern to the plot, the two young men swap identities, participate in jousts, write love-letters, rescue women from sinister assailants, and eventually marry their true loves.

However, *Incognita* is not simply a Restoration comedy removed from the stage to the pages of imaginative fiction: it is a transitional form, somewhere between the prose romances of the seventeenth century and the emerging novel of the eighteenth century. Importantly, Congreve identifies his work as a novel; even more importantly for the purposes of this study, he does so in language that echoes the critical terminology of French *belles lettres*. Congreve's preface thus provides an entry for examining this early and important intersection of rhetorical theory and the novel. I have argued that the relationship of rhetoric and the novel is perhaps most evident in the novel's attempt to resolve the tension between ethics and aesthetics. Congreve identifies this concern in the subtitle of his novel: *Incognita; or, Love and Duty Reconciled*. In *Incognita*, Congreve attempts to reconcile the aesthetics of a traditional romance plot with the ethos of a new genre, though the novel of 1692 is hardly a fixed concept.

Congreve lays out all these concerns in the preface. Though it is only four pages long, Congreve makes note of several features of the novel – both as a genre and his own particular novel – that have specific, direct connections to late seventeenth-century rhetorical theory as well as foreshadowing novel criticism still to come. Specifically, Congreve distances his understanding of the novel from the romance tradition and defines some of the more salient characteristics of the novel genre, using the language of French *belles lettres* to accomplish both tasks. In doing so, he tacitly acknowledges that there is a cultural understanding of a novel genre to which his work might be compared, an understanding that is at least known – if not familiar – to his reader. Furthermore, his deployment of belletristic terminology and concepts concerning the reception of his work implies a similar level of audience familiarity with the language and concepts associated with *belles lettres* rhetorical theory.

The preface begins with Congreve's assertion that he has taken "some little pains" to develop his novel in specific opposition to the romance tradition. The romance, Congreve asserts, generally possesses several traits – both in content and concept – that separate it from his attempt at writing a novel:

> Romances are generally composed of the Constant Loves and invincible Courages of Hero's, Heroins [sic], Kings and Queens, Mortals of the first Rank, and so forth; where lofty Language, miraculous Contingencies and impossible Performances, elevate and surprize [sic] the Reader into a giddy Delight . . . and vexes him to think how he has suffer'd himself to be pleased and transported, concern'd and afflicted at the several Passages which he has Read . . . when he is forced to be very well convinced that 'tis all a lye [sic]. (Congreve, preface to *Incognita*)

Here, Congreve makes note of the outward characteristics of romances, the effect which romances often have on their audiences, and the conceptualization of romances as complete fabrications with little or no relationship to the operation of the real world. This conceptualization of the romance was hardly groundbreaking: the tropes and stylistic characteristics of the romance were well established by 1692, though Congreve slyly insinuates that the romance reader may be looking for imaginative fiction that avoids the more fantastical elements of romance.

Novels, on the other hand, operate in a much different fashion. Novels, Congreve argues, specifically work against many of the romance characteristics he has cited:

> Novels are of a more familiar Nature; Come near us, and represent to us Intrigues in practice, delight us with Accidents and odd Events, but not such as are wholly unusual or unpresidented [sic], such which not being so distant from our Belief bring also the pleasure nearer us. Romances give more Wonder, Novels more Delight. (preface to *Incognita*)

Congreve has here delineated some of the most salient differences between the romance and the novel. Romances are the domain of kings and queens, knights and damsels, heroic deeds and impossible feats of daring and chivalry. Novels are simply "of a more familiar Nature," and this nature includes not only the characters, but the events and the effect of the novel: the plot of a novel may be convoluted and coincidental, but not beyond the realm of possibility; a novel may move the reader, but to delight rather than wonder. Congreve's placement of the novel definition in opposition to the romance tradition is a moment of contextualization and prophecy: his definition of the genre is grounded in his time – the late Restoration – but his definition also looks ahead to future attempts to define the novel genre.

In the genre definition found in the preface to *Incognita* and within the novel itself, Congreve incorporates ideas and language that reverberate with the concept of novelization. Bakhtin's process of novelization points out the tendency of novelistic discourse to emphasize cultural dialogue, humor, irony, parody, and linguistic instability. The awareness of audience expectations found in the preface and *Incognita*'s parody and critique of romance serve to function as moments of novelization. The definition of the novel Congreve builds into the preface seems to indicate a larger sense of the novel's definition shared by the author and audience, perhaps implying a nascent critical language common to seventeenth-century novelist and reader, which would allow this kind of discourse to take place. As I argued earlier in this chapter, novelization's conceptual counterpart in rhetoric is letteraturizzazione, a rhetorical concept that emphasizes the tendency of rhetorical theory to shift in emphasis "from persuasion to narration, from civic to personal contexts, and from speech to literature" (Kennedy 3). The confluence of novelization and *letteraturizzazione* is clearly evident in the discourse shared between Congreve and his audience. This shared discourse, I will argue, is essentially rhetorical in its concerns, with a specifically belletristic framework. Briefly, then, I want to pay close attention to the concepts and ideas Congreve sets forth in order to position them as rhetorical – and specifically belletristic – in their form and function.

To understand how and why Congreve employs belletristic concepts and language, it is first necessary to examine some of the basic principles of French *belles lettres*. Barbara Warnick argues that French rhetoricians of the late seventeenth and early eighteenth century developed a new "sixth canon" of rhetoric in opposition to the classical rhetorical model that included five canons of rhetoric: invention, arrangement, style, delivery, and memory. At various points in the history of rhetoric, the five canons have each assumed more or less importance as the emphasis of different rhetoricians came to bear on the classical concepts. But at the end of the seventeenth century, the expansion of empiricism began to undercut many of the assumptions concerning cognition. By the end of the eighteenth century, Warnick sees invention – one of the five canons of rhetoric in the classical tradition – as replaced by a new, sixth canon: *belles lettres*.

This sixth canon, according to Warnick, was "a fusion of aesthetics and culturally-based psychology" (Warnick 130). Despite such a tidy definition, *belles lettres* as practiced by French rhetoricians – and later rhetoricians of the Scottish enlightenment – is a difficult concept to pin down. Warnick herself describes belletristic rhetorical theory as "heterogenous and complex, sometimes to the point of incoherence" (Warnick 134). As the discussion of Locke has demonstrated, language itself was increasingly seen as an unstable collection of signifiers whose meaning could shift depending on the experiences and contingencies of each reader or listener. Warnick argues that belletristic rhetoric emerged in response to an increasing sense of linguistic instability and represents an attempt to develop a system for analyzing and judging discourse against two primary criteria: propriety and perspicuity. Warnick finds the basis for these two concepts in French critical antecedents.

The discussion of propriety deals first with the French understanding of *bienséance*, an aesthetic term with its origins in social practices which became an important critical concept in the work of François Fenelon (Warnick 50). Warnick argues that propriety was a central concern for all major figures in French *belles lettres*, especially Fenelon. *Bienséance* originally encompassed "social conventions and tacit rules as to what was appropriate in a given social situation" (Warnick 48). This emphasis on *bienséance* served to create ties between ethics and aesthetics, as readers were asked to implement social norms and expectations as criteria for developing an aesthetic sense. As this concept was further absorbed into rhetorical theory, it implied that discourse should focus on clarity and simplicity, avoiding artistic flourishes in favor of concision and unity. In Fenelon's criticism, *bienséance* was understood to refer to the conformity of characters (in drama or poetry) with the social conventions of their era and station in life, as well as whether the action of the characters met the taste and expectations of the audience (Warnick 48). For a work to have *bienséance*, then, it had to meet standards of internal unity and external expectations of the audience. Warnick observes that, regarding aesthetic theory, *bienseance* manifested itself in two ways:

> *Bienseance* had two dimensions – internal and external. Internal application was concerned with whether a character's actions conformed to his rank, profession, age, and situation . . . External application was concerned with whether a depiction conformed to the audience's expectation of what was normal, appropriate, and suited to its taste. (Warnick 48–49)

The concept of *bienseance* thus served a double critical function when assessing fiction. First, *bienseance* allowed the reader to judge the actions of the characters against real-world expectations. For a work to possess *bienseance*, the characters needed to conform to the expected behavior of their rank and position; furthermore, their actions needed to conform to the audience's expectations. Second, the application of *bienseance* to the aesthetic operation of novelistic discourse implies an expectation that language will suit the characters and situations, while presenting the narrative in a clear and precise fashion.

Congreve's understanding of *bienseance* – propriety – is initially evident in his contention that one of the major differences between the romance and the novel is the deployment of language within the novel that is more commonplace and realistic than the lofty and affected language of the romance. In his introduction to the 1922 edition of *Incognita*, H.F.B. Brett-Smith notes that the dialogue of Congreve's novel "has not the magnificent but incessant brilliance of his comedies, and is perhaps for that reason a safer guide to the average level of small talk about the time when the author was twenty-one" (Brett-Smith xiii). Congreve's attention to language and to its suitability to the subject matter and tone of the novel text is thus closely tied to *bienseance*. Brett-Smith's observation, though, is perhaps only valid insofar as it takes note of Congreve's *attempt* to use language that is closer to the "average level of small talk" of Congreve's era. It is difficult to believe that the small talk of Congreve's era closely resembled the dialogue of *Incognita*, seen here as one of the central characters, Aurelian, responds to a simple question about his identity:

> Madam, it is no small demonstration of the entire Resignation which I have made of my heart to your chains, since the secrets of it are no longer in my power. I confess I only took *Florence* in my way, not

designing any longer residence, than should be requisite to inform the Curiosity of a Traveller, of the rarities of the Place. Whether Happiness or Misery will be the Consequence of that Curiosity, I am yet in fear, and submit to your determination; but sure I am, not to depart *Florence* till you have made me the most miserable man in it, and refuse me the fatal Kindness of Dying at your feet. I am by birth a *Spaniard*, of the city of *Toledo*; my name is *Hippolito di Saviolina*. (Congreve 25–26)

This sort of declaration is not at all uncommon in the novel as the characters in *Incognita* engage in verbal jousting which seems to take the place of the physical conflict typical to the romance tradition against which Congreve is consciously working.

Despite such florid dialogue, the content of Aurelian's declaration takes a decidedly novelistic turn in its attention to interiority and intention. In these instances, Congreve's declaration that novels "Come near us, and represent to us Intrigues in practice" (preface to *Incognita*) rings true: the reader is drawn into Aurelian's motivations for concealing his identity and Congreve is careful to describe the characters' decision-making processes. The propriety of such detail – allowing the audience access to the inner workings of the characters – is not necessarily located in Congreve's adherence to a sense of realism, but rather is found within his attention to the unity of Aurelian's character and to the audience's expectations about Aurelian's behavior and actions.

Congreve's implementation of concepts drawn from French *belles lettres* continues throughout the preface as he asserts that novels "delight us with Accidents and odd Events . . . Romances give more Wonder, Novels more Delight" (preface to *Incognita*). The difference between delight and wonder is important: it seems to speak to the intensity of the reader's emotional response. Romances, Congreve argues, evoke an intense emotional response while novels foster delight, a response that is more sustainable because of its lower emotional pitch. This distinction between wonder and delight can be seen in some of the elements of the plot detail. Congreve incorporates plot set pieces that might be more at home in a romance than within his conception of the novel. This is clearly evident in his presentation of the tournament. The two young heroes, Aurelian and Hippolito, true to the romance ideal of chivalry and courtly love, take part in the knightly contests in the service of their ladies: they are equipped with elegant, ornate armor; they unhorse everyone in sight. On the surface, the tournament might seem at home in Malory, yet Congreve contextualizes the tournament in a way that undercuts the romance elements. Congreve is sure to inform the reader that the joust is – in opposition to the jousts of the romance tradition – a ritual intended only for show and that the participants are not in any real danger: "The Cavaliers were all in good earnest, but orders were given to bring 'em blunted Lances, and to forbid the drawing of a Sword upon pain of his Highness's Displeasure" (Congreve 49). Furthermore, Aurelian and Hippolito fail to understand that the presentation of Donna Catharina – the Duke's kinswoman – as the most desirable lady at the tournament was not intended to elicit any real challenges:

> The Exercise which was to be perform'd was in general a running at the Ring, and afterwards two Cavaliers undertook to defend the Beauty of *Donna Catharina*, against all who would not allow her preheminence [sic] of their Mistresses. This thing was only design'd for show and form, none presuming that any Body would put so great an affront upon the Bride and Duke's Kinswoman, as to dispute her pretensions to the first place in the Court of *Venus*. (Congreve 46–47)

When the two young men do challenge her "preheminence" they are restrained by an onlooker, who explains that Donna Catharina's honor was never intended to be disputed.

The confusion of Aurelian and Hippolito seems grounded in their failure to understand how to function as characters in a novel rather than a romance. The tournament highlights the crucial difference between wonder and delight as the reader is invited to find delight in the confusion of the young cavaliers rather than wonder at their martial prowess on the tournament field. Congreve thus takes romance plot elements and renders them novelistic in their execution: the wonder of the romance tradition, located in battles, jousts, enchantments, and quests, devolves into a novelistic interest in delighting the audience and drawing them into storylines that are more familiar and near to their own experiences. In this regard, Congreve is calling into question the aesthetic foundation of the romance: by inviting the audience to laugh at the lack of propriety inherent in many romance conventions, he indicates that the reader should privilege novelistic, rather than romantic, discourse.

In this regard, *Incognita* reflects novelization's emphasis on parody and humor, as Congreve uses the story of four young aristocratic lovers to demonstrate how and why a novel might function differently than romance. Congreve uses romance settings, characters, situations, and tropes, only to point out to the reader the ways in which the novel might be more relevant – or perhaps more aesthetically viable – than the romance. Hammond and Regan assert that Congreve places *Incognita* in opposition "to a form of romance fiction that he brands as both inherently *implausible* and . . . decadently *artificial*" (Hammond and Regan 32). The ideas of plausibility and authenticity – central to many future descriptions of the novel genre – clearly have their roots in French *belles lettres*. As the prior discussion of *bienseance* demonstrates, the importance of authenticity – of characters and situations which are consistent within the framework of the narrative and the experience and expectations of the audience – is evident in both the preface and the text of *Incognita*.

Plausibility, or *vraisemblance*, is also an important concept within French *belles lettres*. Warnick argues that although *bienseance* and *vraisemblance* are closely related, there is a distinct difference:

> [V]*raisemblance* is a broader and more inclusive concept and arises from the congruence of facts and events in a text . . . In its preoccupation with the manner of expression and the artfulness of portrayal, *bienseance* is an aesthetic criterion, whereas verisimilitude [*vraisemblance*] deals with the "logic" of a work. (Warnick 40–41)

These two concepts, crucial to French *belles lettres*, are at the heart of Congreve's definition of the novel in the preface and are evident throughout *Incognita* as he demonstrates how romance does not measure up to either critical concept. As Hammond and Regan observe, the effectiveness of romance narratives in the late seventeenth century begins to falter precisely because of the nature of romance (Hammond and Regan 32). The romance emphasis on fantastical plots and archetypical characters gave way to empiricist concerns with probability and propriety.

Furthermore, as Lennard Davis has observed, *vraisemblance* was a critical concept closely linked with virtue in the eighteenth-century. Davis sees virtue and *vraisemblance* as important to early novelists because of their intended effect on the reader: "[b]oth virtue and verisimilitude are . . . devices to pull a reader hypnotically into the lifeless collections of runes on a page and make the reader create, in effect, the life of characters" (Davis 482). Davis argues that virtue and verisimilitude converge to create cultural norms within early novels:

> [F]rom the point of view of eighteenth-century novelists, virtue and probability are virtually similar although not the same. Virtue is the normative setting for moral definitions of character, while probability is the normative setting for action. Both converge, in effect, in some grand cultural attempt to create normative or average patterns of behaviour. (Davis 482)

Yet I argue that verisimilitude is not only a term used to describe the "normative setting for action" within the early British novel; it is also a rhetorical criterion for judging the artfulness of discourse. Within the belletristic rhetorical conceptions of perspicuity and propriety, the novelistic concerns with the individual and the particular converge with a rhetorical, *letteraturizzazione* emphasis on narrative discourse and personal contexts. If we accept Davis's notion that verisimilitude and virtue were inextricably entwined concepts in the early British novel, we must also come to see such a basis for understanding the novel's development as rhetorical in its expression. Perspicuity and probability, virtue and aesthetics are intricately related novelistic *and* rhetorical concepts that must be understood in relationship to each other.

Thus, the shift in rhetorical theory toward an emphasis on understanding and judging discourse that found expression in French *belles lettres* marked a profound change in the way literature and art were perceived and understood. The sixth canon's focus on perspicuity and propriety created the basis for future standards of judging literature which continued to resonate throughout the eighteenth century and on into the nineteenth. In this regard, *Incognita* is transitional as Congreve sets about appropriating rhetorical aesthetic concepts for the purposes of literary criticism *and* literary production. Congreve's definition of the novel in the preface to *Incognita* is founded on rhetorical concepts: the insistence on *bienseance* and the distinction between wonder and delight are ideas predicated on a *belles lettres* rhetorical understanding of the novel. Though the subject matter of the novel seems grounded in the romance tradition, Congreve's conceptualization of the novel draws clear distinctions between the novel and romance, distinctions that can only be made through the implementation of belletristic rhetorical concepts.

Yet the *belles lettres* found in Congreve's novel is somewhat distanced from the Scottish *belles lettres* we will encounter in the latter half of the eighteenth century. While the French rhetoricians who worked in *belles lettres* clearly understood the analytical dimension of rhetoric, their work did little to alter the classical conception of virtue. In the end, the conceptualization of virtue at the heart of *Incognita* is still a classical concept, tied to birth and breeding. But this understanding of virtue would soon undergo an important change. In *The Age of Virtue,* David Morse argues that the classical understanding of virtue that dominated the Restoration and early eighteenth century was based on the Aristotelian concept, found in his *Nicomachean Ethics*, of "the soldier as citizen and the citizen as soldier, where the most highly valued qualities are courage, self-discipline, and prudence" (Morse 3). As the eighteenth century unfolded, this conception of virtue was giving way to another model that emphasized the public good, benevolence, and correct behavior. Morse asserts that while these qualities were still understood, ideally, to be found in the aristocracy, there was a growing belief throughout the eighteenth century that virtue might be more readily located in the lower strata of society:

> [S]trangely, although virtue was generally perceived as the prerogative of aristocrats and gentlemen, there were few indeed who actually believed that such pampered and indulged individuals were likely to be virtuous. Indeed, the whole history of the novel, from Richardson and Fielding to Jane Austen, is based on the idea that if you want virtue you should look

to the lowly, whether without fortune, feminine, illegitimate or actually servants – these are the only people you can rely on. (Morse 24)

From here, Morse's argument about the various permutations of virtue throughout the eighteenth century traces its way through politics and education and philosophy. But his identification of the novel as the location where virtue was revised and rediscovered is important. Early proto-novels like *Incognita* or Behn's *Oroonoko* still located virtue in birth and breeding: the young men and women at the center of Congreve's novel are aristocrats, and Oroonoko's virtue is demonstrated in his nobility in the face of terrible circumstances.

The novelistic infusion of virtue with a sense of broad societal moral expectations was to come later and find expression in the work of Defoe, Richardson, and Fielding. These authors developed novels that demonstrated the transformation of virtue from an aristocratic concept to a culturally shared, egalitarian moral sense. The development of a discourse concerning moral sense in the fiction of Defoe, Richardson, and Fielding is well-traveled territory; however, understanding this transformation of virtue as rhetorical in its conception – while decidedly novelistic in its expression – is perhaps less familiar. Yet as we shall see, eighteenth-century rhetoricians, exploring how this new understanding of virtue might be inculcated in the masses, increasingly turned to contemporary examples rather than classical models. This is not to say that classical models were abandoned; rather, the classical was augmented by the contemporary. As the question of developing a shared cultural sense of virtue evolved, scholars and intellectuals began to look to the novel despite any perceived aesthetic and moral shortcomings. Novels like *Robinson Crusoe* and *Pamela* offered a new vision of virtue, unfettered from aristocratic moorings. Looking to the end of the eighteenth century, we will see that rhetoricians associated with Scottish *belles lettres* began to turn to novels to synthesize their conception of aesthetics and moral purpose. Conversely, as some of the earliest comprehensive histories of the novel began to emerge at the end of the eighteenth century, *belles lettres* was increasingly utilized in explaining the novel's potential for developing a cohesive, national sense of morality and virtue.

Chapter 4
Belles Lettres Rhetoric, the Novel, and the "Horizon of Expectation"

> *Let me, therefore, prepare for disappointment those who, in the perusal of these sheets, entertain the gentle expectation of being transported to the fantastic regions of Romance, where Fiction is coloured by all the gay tints of luxurious Imagination, where Reason is an outcast, and where the sublimity of the Marvellous rejects all aid from sober Probability.*
>
> Fanny Burney, Preface to Evelina

The Novel Reading Public at the End of the Eighteenth Century

In the preface and dedication to her first novel, *Evelina* (1778), Frances Burney makes an appeal to two different audiences. At the end of the preface, she states that *Evelina* is presented to "the public – for such, by novel writers, novel readers will be called" (Burney xii). Burney also makes an appeal to another group of readers. She begins by addressing the "Authors of the Monthly and Critical Reviews" and requests from them, simultaneously, leniency and justice in their evaluation of her literary efforts:

> Without name, without recommendation, and unknown alike to success and disgrace, to whom can I so properly apply for patronage, as to those who publicly profess themselves Inspectors of all literary performances?
>
> The extensive plan of your critical observations, which, not confined to works of utility or ingenuity, is equally open to those of frivolous amusement . . . encourages me to seek for your protection . . . To resent, therefore, this offering, however insignificant, would ill become the universality of your undertaking; though not to despise it may, alas! be out of your power. (Burney vi)

Burney clearly sees her audiences as interrelated. She acknowledges that her own novels – and novels as a genre – are primarily intended for a broad readership throughout the reading public. But she is also well aware that a body of critics – the "Inspectors of all literary performance" and the "Magistrates of the press . . . Censors for the public" (Burney vii) – is interposed between her novel and her public audience. Thus, the seventeen-year-old, self-educated Burney feels it necessary to advocate directly to her potential critics on behalf of her anonymous novel.

Burney demonstrates a keen awareness of the genre's critical status at the end of the eighteenth century. She begins by acknowledging the majority of novels are not held in high esteem by critics and the genre is only redeemed by authors like Rousseau, Johnson[1], Marivaux, Fielding, Richardson, and Smollett. She then stakes out her novel's territory, particularly in opposition to the Romance:

> Let me, therefore, prepare for disappointment those who, in the perusal of these sheets, entertain the gentle expectation of being transported to the fantastic regions of Romance, where Fiction is coloured by all the gay tints of luxurious Imagination, where Reason is an outcast, and where the sublimity of the Marvellous rejects all aid from sober Probability. (Burney *Preface*)

Like Congreve a century earlier, Burney has set her novel apart from the "fantastic regions of Romance" and places it instead within the realm of familiar life through the invocation of the belletristic concept of probability.

Burney's conceptualization of critics, readers, and the novel is important within a discussion of novel history, rhetoric, and criticism for several reasons. First, Burney tells us that in the latter part of the eighteenth century there was an established, recognizable body of professional critics concerned with developing critical judgments about novels on behalf of the public. Second, Burney strongly intimates that novel readers are found throughout all strata of society and that this public, in some ways, relies on the judgments of the critics in creating its own literary assessments. Third, the definition of the novel is still understood primarily in its difference from the romance; importantly, this difference – as in Congreve's 1692 definition – is expressed in the critical language of *belles lettres*[2].

Burney's clear desire to interact with both her critical and public reading audiences using a critical language grounded in belletristic rhetoric is an indication that novel readers had a particular set of expectations about the novels they read. And while Burney's request for mercy from her readers is perhaps unique, invoking and instructing the novel-reading audience in prefaces, introductions, and even in-text was a hallmark of eighteenth-century fiction. Eighteenth-century novelists directly addressed the audience for a host of reasons: Aphra Behn, in *Oroonoko*, and Daniel Defoe, in *Robinson Crusoe*, for example, attempt to establish the supposed historicity of their narratives; in *Pamela*, Samuel Richardson outlines the didactic purpose of his text, while Fielding establishes a critical paradigm for reading *Joseph Andrews*. Garrett Stewart argues that any direct address to the reader of a text is "the site of an

---

[1] Johnson, of course, was one of the critics Burney was appealing to for mercy.
[2] As demonstrated in the previous chapter, probability was a central concept in the emergence of *belles lettres* as a system of criticism.

implicated response, however minimal, by which the reading subject is gradually taken for granted in the narrative text, granted to it and so assumed by it, assumed and presumed upon" (Stewart 27). William St. Clair is somewhat more succinct when he describes the preconceptions brought to texts by readers of the romantic period as their "horizons of expectation" (St. Clair 4-5). Furthermore, St. Clair asserts that these expectations are central to understanding the impact of texts within their cultural contexts:

> We may confidently accept the existence of 'communities of interpretation' who bring shared preconceptions and expectations about texts and genres to the act of reading, and accept as a premise that readers were normally much constrained in the meanings they created and accepted. We may reasonably assume too that strategies were often successful in pre-setting expectations and responses, and that some readers may have devoted considerable efforts to trying to build a full and balanced critical understanding... of the texts which they read. (St. Clair 4–5).

St. Clair's invocation of the horizon of expectation for readers of the romantic period is drawn from the work of Hans Robert Jauss, who argues that "[t]he coherence of literature as an event is primarily mediated in the horizon of expectation of the literary experience of contemporary and later readers, critics, and authors" (Jauss 166).

Jauss asserts that any meaningful literary history must be predicated on an understanding of how texts carry with themselves a horizon of expectation that is constantly revised as the text is read by successive generations of readers and critics. This horizon of expectation can either support or challenge the status quo: some texts function by "precisely fulfilling the expectations prescribed by a ruling standard of taste," while works that oppose the ruling standard of taste eventually revise the horizon of expectation and "[enter] into the horizon of future aesthetic experience" (Jauss 169). Eighteenth-century rhetoric provided a perfect vehicle for creating such a horizon of expectation. Lloyd Bitzer argues that rhetorical inquiry is concerned with establishing correct judgment; furthermore, "rhetoric generates truths and values previously unknown to a public, gives voice to interests and principles whose locus is a public, serves as an instrument with which to test public truths and values and to select and justify public means and ends" (Bitzer 68). Bitzer's understanding of rhetoric succinctly sums up the reasons rhetoric, especially as expressed in Hugh Blair's belletristic approach, provided an ideal vehicle for articulating and disseminating a particular horizon of expectation throughout the reading public of nineteenth-century British literary culture. In this chapter, I will describe the horizon of expectation for novel-readers of the late eighteenth and early nineteenth century, arguing that belletristic rhetoric, typified in the work of Hugh Blair, played a crucial role in developing such expectations about the novel-reading experience.

While the previous chapter focused on an examination of Congreve's *Incognita* and its accompanying preface as a way to demonstrate and understand the presence of belletristic rhetorical concepts in the earliest stages of the British novel's development, the current chapter will focus on the concluding decades of the eighteenth century. This is not meant to indicate a lull in the development of the novel or novel criticism during the years between Congreve's *Incognita* and the end of the eighteenth century. But since this study attempts to understand the relationship between *belles lettres* rhetoric and the development of novel criticism, it may be useful to move to the latter part of the eighteenth century and the early nineteenth in order to closely examine how rhetorical theory influenced the expectations of novel readers at the end of the century.

During the latter part of the eighteenth century, rhetoric continued its transformation from a generative to an analytical discipline. *Belles lettres* rhetoric's continuing emphasis on developing critical judgment was tied to the expansion of literacy and an increase in the availability of inexpensive reading material. The combination of increasing literacy and inexpensive reading material was viewed by the existing literate culture[3] as alarming for several interrelated reasons. The spread of literacy among the lower classes was often blamed for fostering social unrest and political upheaval; as the century closed, widespread literacy was often cast as playing a central role in allowing the horrors of the French Revolution to unfold. Less terrifying, but understood to be just as dangerous, was the thought of what the newly literate masses might choose for their reading material. As Richard Altick argues, "the growth of the reading public was viewed with an alarm originating largely in concern for the individual reader's personal morality" and much of this concern focused on novels (Altick 66). Literacy was thus viewed in some quarters as potentially harmful to a mass reading public not possessed of the education or experience to make proper and discerning choices about their leisure reading.

Belletristic rhetoric, with its civic-minded emphasis on the individual's development of taste and judgment, stepped into the breach. Thomas P. Miller contends that while the established literate classes were deeply apprehensive about the new reading public, this body of new readers and the explosion of cheap, available reading material "provided a domain where the middle classes could develop a critical understanding of their social experience" (Miller 32). Thus, Miller argues, the critical function of rhetoric "became a means to instill

---

[3] Here I am referring to those elements in British society that did not become newly literate at this time. This might include the aristocracy, landed gentry, ecclesiastical classes, and the educated upper-middle class of lawyers, bankers, and merchants.

taste as the reading public expanded" (Miller 32); furthermore, rhetoric's continuing shift from production to analysis caused rhetoric to assume the role of "a critical enterprise concerned with instilling appropriate moral sentiments and aesthetic responses" (Miller 180). While Miller argues that developing proper taste and judgment was a pathway for the newly literate masses – and especially, the newly literate populations of Ireland and Scotland – to access dominant English cultural ideals, Marjorie Garson asserts just the opposite, contending that the invocation of taste and judgment often drew stark lines between the cultural elite and the aspiring masses:

> Implying that 'taste,' which is fully available to non-aristocratic, middle-class individuals but that these individuals must 'cultivate' themselves in order to acquire it, the metaphor speaks to the ambition of those who feel they have both the energy to undertake such cultivation and the innate superiority that will make their efforts pay off. (Garson 14)

Clearly, then, the concept of taste, coupled with the invocation of judgment, was crucial to the development of aesthetic systems during the eighteenth – and, as Garson argues – the nineteenth centuries. And while taste and judgment received attention from intellectuals such as Edmund Burke, David Hume, Lord Shaftesbury, and Francis Hutcheson (Garson 5-6), the standards and methods for developing taste and judgment were communicated to the more general public through the work of rhetoricians.

These crosscurrents of rhetoric, morality, and aesthetics became crucial elements in the development of novel histories and criticism at the turn of the eighteenth century. Richard Altick asserts that "the ordinary novel, more than any other form of literature, helped democratize reading in the eighteenth century," a process that "touched off the first widespread discussion of the social effects of a democratized reading audience" (Altick 63). Altick further contends that "[t]he popular reading audience owed its birth in large part to the novel" (Altick 65). Altick's assertions about the novel and the new reading public cast Miller's observations about the increasingly critical function of rhetoric in a very specific light, and in this chapter I argue that if belletristic rhetorical theory was intended to instill "appropriate moral sentiments and aesthetic responses" (Miller 180) in this new body of readers, much of that work would necessarily be done in relationship to the novel.

Mid-Century Appraisals of the Novel

Yet before examining the horizon of novel-reading expectation at the end of the eighteenth century, it is necessary to at least briefly examine the development of the novel and novel criticism through the eighteenth century. The middle of the eighteenth century is often seen as the high point of the early British novel, and Watt's trinity of Defoe, Richardson, and Fielding had all written their major works. Though there was still some disagreement about just what to call this new vein of imaginative fiction, critics, authors, and readers all acknowledged that the prose fiction of the first half of the eighteenth century was somehow different from the prose fiction of prior eras.

The increase in production and readership of novels at this time brought about critical assessments of a genre that was still fighting for respectability. In broad terms, the novel was seen as potentially dangerous for two reasons. First, the novel was perceived as potentially dangerous in its ability to present vice as seductive and attractive, especially to young women. Much of this scrutiny focused on French novels, but the questionable nature of the genre extended into novels of every nationality: in the preface to *Constantia* (1751), for example, the anonymous author observes that while Italian novels are full of wit and charm, they are also often concerned with "indecent intrigues," thus rendering these novels "improper for the perusal of young people" (preface to *Constantia* vi). Even works that consciously praised virtue and condemned vice were subject to scrutiny and cautionary advice (McKeon 602).

Second, the novel – or more precisely, novel *reading* – was seen in many circumstances to be an idle frivolity, distracting the readers from their duties or from activities of a more improving nature. An obvious example is found in *Gulliver's Travels* when the Lilliputian Queen's maid falls asleep reading a romance (a term at this time not necessarily synonymous with "novel," but often enough used interchangeably) and burns down part of the palace. Whatever else is to be made of Swift's skewering of leisure reading, there was clearly an eighteenth-century concern that an increase in leisure reading within the rapidly broadening reading public would lead to idleness, sloth, and the dereliction of vocational duty throughout the lower classes. Richard Altick cites numerous examples from nineteenth-century British periodicals of the presence of a "national legend" concerning the evils of easily available novels. Novels were blamed for housewives and clerks abandoning their responsibilities to pursue a passion for novel-reading. At least one critic went so far as to claim that he would rather see young men frequenting public houses than public libraries (Altick 232-233). Altick argues that this reaction to the spread of reading in the eighteenth century was closely tied to the spread of novel reading: during the eighteenth century there developed a "rigid, ineffaceable association of the mass reading public with low-grade fiction" (Altick 64). The results of such an association were primarily understood in a most unfavorable light:

> All who opposed the spread of literacy among the common people found their worst fears realized. Here, they said, was proof enough of what happened when people who had no business reading – women and domestic servants in particular – turned to books: they cultivated

habits of idleness and lost themselves in unwholesome, overheated dreams (Altick 64).

Most fiction occupied an exceptionally low status in the minds of the literate elite: Altick states that the majority of circulating-library novels were perceived as "innocuous [at best] but oftener frivolous and even licentious" (Altick 65). The perception of the novel as an idle and illicit pastime for domestics and young women made it an easy target for criticism on moral and religious grounds, though as John Tinnon Taylor observes, many of these objections were offered by "those who never read anything but novels" (Taylor 7). Yet objections of this sort point less to widespread hypocrisy about reading novels and more toward the belief that the lower classes, as newly literate readers, lacked the experience and education to critically read and form proper judgments about novels.

Samuel Johnson takes on just this problem in *The Rambler* Volume I, number 4. In this essay, dated March 31, 1750, Johnson attempts to explain the aesthetic and ethical purpose of fiction. He begins by noting the ever-expanding popularity of a new fiction[4] that concerns itself with "life in its true state" (Johnson, *The Rambler* 18). This new fiction – Johnson never uses the term "novel" – attempts to present an accurate picture of common, day-to-day life:

> The works of fiction, with which the present generation seems more particularly delighted, exhibit life in its true state, diversified only by accidents that happen daily in the world, and influenced by passions and qualities which are really to be found in conversing with mankind. (Johnson, *The Rambler* 18)

Johnson continues his definition by succinctly summing up the goals of the present vein of fiction, claiming that "[i]ts province is to bring about natural events by easy means, and to keep up curiosity without the help of wonder" (18). This last statement clearly resonates with Congreve's argument sixty years earlier that novels arouse delight in the reader, while romance creates wonder. Johnson's emphasis on natural events brought about through easy means is also clearly rhetorical as he evokes belletristic concerns for propriety and verisimilitude.

Johnson's tone is dismissive of the romance tradition as he paints with a broad brush, scoffing that "almost all fictions of the past age will vanish, if you deprive them of a hermit and a wood, a battle and a shipwreck" (18). This sort of fiction, according to Johnson, is contemptible in its failure to depict real life;

---

[4] Johnson's reference to new fiction primarily encompasses the prior half century or so and is clearly intended to be understood in opposition to older prose fictions, particularly romance.

furthermore, the authors of such fiction write with little artistic merit, producing books "without fear of criticism, without the toil of study, without knowledge of nature, or acquaintance with life" (19). The break between prior prose fiction and contemporary prose fiction is clear to Johnson: while romance authors relied upon the fantastical and fanciful, contemporary novelists look to the commonplace and everyday.

In Johnson's opinion, this renders the work of the novelist much more difficult. Because the subjects of novels are drawn from familiar life, novels are observed more closely by an audience able to "detect any deviation from exactness of resemblance:"

> The task of our present writers is very different [from that of romance writers]; it requires, together with that learning which is to be gained from books, that experience that can never be attained by solitary diligence, but must arise from general converse and accurate observation of the living world . . . Other writings are safe, except from the malice of learning, but these are in danger from every common reader. (Johnson, *The Rambler* 19)

Johnson, like Burney three decades later, understands there are two distinct audiences reading and responding to novels. The aesthetics of the novel – the attention to detail and the adherence to a sense of propriety in relation to the depiction of the actual world – are thus subject to the criticism of both professional critics (through "the malice of learning") and a reading public that, according to Johnson, has a clear horizon of expectation about the nature and substance of the novel.

But aesthetic expectations are only one facet of the challenge presented to novelists. Johnson argues that, in addition to the aesthetic demands of the genre, novelists must be especially careful to consider the moral and ethical ramifications of their fiction. The power of this new fiction lies in its adherence to real life, and Johnson indicates that artful depictions of virtue and vice can influence readers in ways other forms of literature simply do not. This concern is magnified for Johnson because of his conception of the novel's target audience:

> These books are written chiefly to the young, the ignorant, and the idle, to whom they serve as lectures of conduct, and introductions to life. They are the entertainment of minds unfurnished with ideas, and therefore easily susceptible of impressions; not fixed by fancy, and therefore easily following the current of fancy; not informed by experience, and consequently open to every false suggestion and partial account. (Johnson, *The Rambler* 19)

While his assumption that novels primarily target "the young, the ignorant, and the idle" is unfounded, Johnson's admiration for the aesthetic aims of the novel is clearly tempered by his misgivings over the genre's possible effect on its audience. Yet despite his concern about the potential for harm in novel reading, Johnson regards fiction as one of the best possible venues for teaching readers to pursue virtue and shun vice: "[T]hese familiar histories may be made of greater use than the solemnities of professed morality, and convey the knowledge of vice and virtue with more efficacy than axioms and definitions" (Johnson, *The Rambler* 20).

Johnson's cautious enthusiasm is one of the more salient features of the body of criticism espoused by the "Inspectors of all literary performance" and "censors for the Public" referred to by Burney in her preface to *Evelina*. As Michael McKeon has observed, "the maxim that morals ... are best taught through fables (or examples) was a commonplace in eighteenth-century novel theory" (McKeon, *Origins of the English Novel* 600). An early example is found in the 1715 translation of Pierre-Daniel Huet's *The History of Romances*. Huet's translator, Stephen Lewis, argues in the preface to Huet's *History* that popular fiction emerged as a means of instruction. Lewis claims that the original purpose of the prose romance was:

> to mollify the Rigour of Precepts, by the Allurements of Example. Where the Mind can't be subdued into Virtue, by Reason and Philosophy, nothing can influence it more, than to present to it the Success and Felicity, which Crowns the Pursuit of what's Great and Honourable ... And since in all Ages there were very few real Instances, fit to be proposed for Exact Patterns of Imitation; the Ingenious Fabulist was forced to supply them out of his own Invention. (Lewis, *Preface* ii – iii)

Arguments like those offered by Lewis became part of the critical understanding of the novel that emerged during the eighteenth century. Lewis's understanding of fables and romance is also firmly rooted in classical rhetorical theory, as his assertion that there are few factual instances which provide perfect examples for instruction clearly echoes Aristotle's discussion of enthymeme, maxim, and example found in Book II of his *Rhetoric* (221–236; bk. II, ch. XX–XXV).

Such eighteenth-century endorsements for the didactic power of fiction abound: in the preface to *Constantia*, published in 1751, the anonymous author echoes Johnson's qualified praise for the novel, arguing that most people are unlikely to read anything at all, and when they do pick up reading material, the text is most likely chosen for amusement. Thus, "books of amusement alone have a chance of coming into their hands, and consequently of producing an alteration in such tempers" (Preface to *Constantia* iv). Much later, in his 1797 preface to Smollett's collected works, John Moore argues that novels "may be written with as moral an intention, and contain as many excellent rules for the conduct of life, as any book with a more solemn and scientific title" (Moore xciii – xciv). This idea is put into much stronger terms in Anna Letitia Barbauld's 1810 *Essay on the Origin and Progress of Novel Writing*, when she asserts that novels have the power to shape national character: "Let me make the novels of a country, and let who will make the systems" (Barbauld 59). This line of defense for novel reading continued well into the nineteenth century: in 1832, for example, Harriet Martineau maintained that Walter Scott's effect on the morality of his readers is greater than the combined influence of all the clergy (both Anglican and dissenting), all the teachers at all the universities, and all contemporary philosophers (Martineau 25-27).

While Samuel Johnson clearly sees the novel as artistically superior to the romance, he still fears that the aesthetic strengths of the genre pose a potential danger to readers who lack sufficient education or experience to recognize the difference between virtue and vice. The novel's artistic achievements are at the root of the problem: Johnson argues that prose romances have a minor effect on the reader's sense of propriety and virtue because the romance is "so remote from all that passes among men, that the reader [is] in very little danger of making any applications to himself" (Johnson, *The Rambler* 20). The new prose fiction, however, approaches much closer to actual lived experience, making it that much more dangerous for inexperienced and uneducated readers:

> [W]hen an adventurer is levelled [sic] with the rest of the world, and acts in such scenes of the universal drama, as may be the lot of any other man; young spectators fix their eyes upon him with close attention, and hope, by observing his behaviour and success, to regulate their own practices, when they shall be engaged in the like part. (Johnson, *The Rambler* 20)

Thus, reading fiction during the latter half of the eighteenth century was increasingly seen as a venture fraught with possibility and peril. Novels could inculcate virtue while demonstrating the perils of vice, but even the best-written novels with the purest intentions could lead impressionable readers astray if those readers lacked the experience and education required to make correct critical judgments about these novelistic presentations of virtue and vice.

One of the more memorable fictional examples of this kind of reader is Catherine Morland, the inexperienced and naïve heroine of Jane Austen's *Northanger Abbey*. Throughout the first half of the novel, Austen systematically establishes Catherine's affinity for romance and gothic fiction while emphasizing her complete lack of guile and experience. Catherine's innate good sense serves her well as she navigates the unfamiliar waters of the Bath social scene, but when she removes to the Tilney estate at Northanger Abbey, she ceases to rely on her own judgment and begins to turn almost entirely to a worldview informed by gothic fiction of the late eighteenth-century, especially Ann Radcliffe's *Mysteries of Udolpho* and M.G. Lewis's *The Monk*. Catherine, under the influence of the melancholy abbey and her passion for gothic fiction, begins to interpret the

Tilney family's actions and words as if she were in the plot of a gothic novel. She reaches the entirely unsupportable conclusion that General Tilney cruelly mistreated and then murdered his wife and is only dissuaded when Henry Tilney forces her to examine her assertion in the light of her own common sense:

> Dear Miss Morland, consider the dreadful nature of the suspicions you have entertained. What have you been judging from? Remember the country and age in which we live. Remember that we are English: that we are Christians. Consult your own understanding, your own sense of the probable, your own observation of what is passing around you . . . Dearest Miss Morland, what ideas have you been admitting? (Austen 137)

Henry's argument carries additional force with Catherine because of his own familiarity with the gothic genre. During a conversation with Catherine in Bath, Tilney admits that he generally does not like novels, calling the majority "the stupidest things in creation" while admitting a fondness for M.G. Lewis's *The Monk*: "Novels are so full of nonsense and stuff! There has not been a tolerably decent one come out since *Tom Jones*, except *The Monk*" (Austen 30). So while Henry and Catherine share an appreciation for novels, Henry is better equipped to read them critically: he is well-educated, well-traveled, and well-read. His experience and education allow him to read and enjoy Radcliffe, Lewis, and the other gothic writers without endangering his judgment.

Austen's attention to the question of female reading, specifically regarding the novel, is perhaps best understood in relationship to Thomas Gisborne's *Enquiry into the Duties of the Female Sex* (1797). As Robert Uphaus observes, Austen wrote Northanger Abbey during 1797-1798, just after the publication of Gisborne's *Enquiry* (Uphaus 334). Gisborne's conduct manual presents a damning assessment of novel reading as a pastime for young women: novel reading is habit-forming, and the taste for novels soon becomes "too keen to be denied" (Gisborne 216). According to Gisborne, young women who read novels soon find their morals and standards eroded, and "[w]hat would formerly have given offence, now gives none. The palate is vitiated or made dull . . . [and novels] are devoured with indiscriminate and insatiable avidity" (Gisborne 217). Uphaus argues that Gisborne's attack on novel reading was far from singular: "Gisborne was not so much initiating as summarizing the negative view of women as consumers of fiction. From the mid-eighteenth century onwards there occurs a steady attack on women as the principal readers of fiction" (Uphaus 336).

William Warner argues that during the late eighteenth century novels were viewed as dangerous to young women like Austen's Catherine Morland on precisely the grounds stated by Gisborne, and asserts that in eighteenth-century appraisals of the genre "[t]he power and danger of novels, especially to young women not exposed to classical education, arises from the pleasures novels induce" (Warner 5); furthermore, St. Clair asserts that there was a widely-held cultural suspicion of reading as a leisure activity for young women:

> [Reading was] seen as one of the biggest threats to the existing social structures. Some [critics and moralizers] distrust almost all reading. Others urge their readers, especially women and young people, to be moderate in the amount of reading they indulge in, choose carefully what to read . . . Reading should be undertaken in moderation and under supervision. Women were at risk of liking reading too much. It was too exciting, too distracting, and it inflamed the imagination. Women were liable to become literature abusers, with disastrous consequences for themselves, their families, and society at large. (St. Clair 280–281)

Barbauld offers just this sort of advice in 1825, when she praises the novel as a vehicle for communicating "sentiment and morals" to young women but cautions them to choose their reading material with "great care and the advice of . . . older friends" (Barbauld 43).

Austen indicates that this is exactly Catherine's problem: without anyone to guide her reading, her limited perspective makes novel reading potentially dangerous, though the danger might be remedied with time and experience. The supposed danger of novel reading was not limited to young women: in Thomas Love Peacock's gothic satire, *Nightmare Abbey* (1818), young Scythrop Glowry becomes melancholy and overly dramatic after he spends too much time reading German romances and gothic fiction. Scythrop constructs secret passages and hidden rooms and threatens (though comically fails to attempt) suicide when he is disappointed in love. Scythrop, though well-educated, shares with Catherine Morland a lack of the necessary experience that would allow him to make correct judgments about how to act in response to his reading material.

The inability of young readers like Catherine Morland and Scythrop Glowry to properly respond to reading gothic fiction highlights a question Richard Altick asserts became a central focus in nineteenth-century arguments about the place of the novel within British culture: while novels might make a powerful and positive impression upon readers, there existed a definite prospect for harm if the reader was too inexperienced or uneducated to properly respond to novelistic portrayals of virtue and vice. This anxiety led to a pursuit of how to best make reading safe (Altick 76). As Mr. Flosky[5] laments in *Nightmare Abbey*, "'How can we [the literate cultural elite] be cheerful, when we are surrounded

---

[5] In Peacock's satire of melancholy German romances and gothic novels, Mr. Flosky is a satiric characterization of Samuel Taylor Coleridge.

by a *reading public*, that is growing too wise for its betters?'" (Peacock 113). The answer, it turns out, was *belles lettres* rhetoric.

Belles Lettres Rhetoric and a Novel Reading Horizon of Expectation

As the newest segment of literate society continued to emerge at the end of the eighteenth century, the threat to existing social structures posed by reading loomed large. St. Clair argues that in response, political, ecclesiastical, and educational leaders began to look for a way to construct an acceptable set of fixed cultural attitudes:

> During the romantic period . . . leaders devoted a good deal of effort to identifying, devising, and describing a culture which they believed was appropriate to the times, and which they wished to see diffused and applied through the nation's political, religious, judicial, educational, and other opinion-forming institutions. (St. Clair 269)

Rhetorical theory naturally became central to this effort. Because of rhetoric's emphasis on the moral and ethical dimensions of discourse and because of the widespread dissemination of rhetorical training within eighteenth-century British culture, the critical language used to describe the purpose, function, and aesthetics of the novel took on specifically rhetorical dimensions. The examination of early statements about the novel, such as Congreve's preface to *Incognita*, demonstrate the presence of belletristic rhetorical concepts in conceptualizations of how the novel functioned; as the eighteenth century progressed, *belles lettres* rhetoric played a crucial role in instructing and informing novel readers about how to understand and judge a novel.

At the close of the eighteenth century, defending the novel necessarily became a two-part process. To be taken seriously, novels needed to be well-written and well-conceived; novels needed to conform to a two-part aesthetic model of *bienseance* (propriety) and *vraisemblance* (verisimilitude and probability) that was demonstrably rooted in *belles lettres*. But the aesthetic effect of a novel was nullified if the text did not have an equally demonstrable moral and ethical basis. Moral content became a crucial element in the development of eighteenth-century imaginative fiction: as Edward Pitcher has observed, "[i]n the early eighteenth century, authors deliberately sought to fuse a new narrative style and fictional content with an ancient narrative purpose: there was a marriage of realism to didacticism" (Pitcher 200). This interrelationship became the focus of novel criticism throughout the latter half of the eighteenth century and into the nineteenth century. Increasingly, though, it became clear that simply linking the aesthetic and moral dimensions of the genre was not enough to make novel reading safe: readers needed to be taught how to make the correct kinds of critical judgments about novels, both as aesthetic and ethical objects.

The rhetorical basis for much of the literary criticism of the nineteenth century is not difficult to demonstrate, yet it is often overlooked. James Engell argues that the British rhetoricians of the late eighteenth century (Engell calls them "New Rhetoricians") constitute a cohesive and influential body of critics whose influence extended into "the Romantic veneration of the expressive and emotional power of figurative . . . language" and beyond:

> The New Rhetoricians, properly considered a unified movement, are, prior to the twentieth century, the most important and cohesive group of critics in English. The appeal of their lectures and volumes, often used as texts on both sides of the Atlantic, lasted into Queen Victoria's reign. (Engell 217)

Engell's assertion about the importance of rhetoric in the development of criticism in the eighteenth and nineteenth centuries is no revelation to rhetoric scholars and historians of literary criticism, but the impact on the history of the British novel is perhaps less obvious and well-known.

Miller maintains that contemporary literary scholars generally begin their histories of the discipline in the nineteenth century with accounts of historical philology initializing the professionalization of English studies at Oxford and Cambridge. However, Miller argues that such histories are incomplete because of the role eighteenth-century rhetoricians played in the solidification of literary studies:

> Rhetoricians were the first professors to teach English literature and composition, but when literary studies became professionalized in the nineteenth century, scholarship on rhetoric began to be marginalized as the discipline came to concentrate on philological studies and a few literary genres – poetry, drama, and fiction. (Miller 3)

Yet the place of rhetoric within the history of English as an academic discipline, within the development of literary criticism, and as the critical lens for readers of every social stratum to understand and respond to the British novel of the eighteenth and nineteenth centuries is undeniable.

Engell's assertion about the place of the New Rhetoricians as the most important, cohesive, and clearly identifiable body of critics prior to the twentieth century focuses on names familiar to rhetoric scholars, including Lord Kames, Adam Smith, James Beattie, George Campbell, and Hugh Blair. Most of these figures, however, are often ignored or dismissed within literary histories. Of these figures, only Adam Smith[6] is widely studied outside of rhetoric scholarship. While his

---

[6] Smith's influence as a rhetorician during the eighteenth century was perhaps limited primarily to the educated elite. Smith began his lecture series in 1748, but requested the

Theory of Moral Sentiments and *The Wealth of Nations* were important and influential statements of eighteenth-century moral and political philosophy, his position as the first Professor of Rhetoric and Belles Lettres at the University of Glasgow is perhaps just as significant. As Miller observes, "Smith created one of the first university courses on English literature, composition, and rhetoric . . . Smith and other Scottish moral philosophers such as David Hume and Thomas Reid mapped out the discursive domain within which English was first constituted as an object of study in the university" (Miller 24). Smith's position as a professor of English and a major figure in eighteenth-century moral philosophy is noteworthy: according to Miller, eighteenth-century moral philosophy shared many concerns with rhetoric:

> [L]ike rhetoric, moral philosophy has traditionally been involved in projecting the authority of the educated into the public domain – the domain where questions about moral authority and personal identity take on practical political significance . . . In this domain intellectual inquiry becomes practically involved with the popular experience. (Miller 8)

The intersection of the educated elite and the newly literate public, as described by Michael McKeon, raised questions about the nature of truth and virtue that were central to the development of the British novel. Miller's assertion about moral philosophy's attempt to project the authority of the educated classes into the larger public domain perfectly describes the development of novel criticism and the horizon of expectation for novel readers at the end of the eighteenth century.

As stated at the chapter's outset, rhetoric was the ideal vehicle for creating and disseminating a novelistic horizon of expectation at the end of the eighteenth century. The widespread influence of rhetorical education in Britain during the latter half of the eighteenth century perhaps needs no further explanation. But rhetoric's role in creating horizons of expectation goes far beyond its cultural pervasiveness. Lloyd Bitzer's exploration of rhetoric's relationship to public knowledge provides concise and cogent insights into rhetoric's ability to create, develop, maintain, and support cultural norms and values. Bitzer claims that rhetoric "seeks to establish correct judgments" (Bitzer 68); furthermore,

> [R]hetoric generates truths and values previously unknown to a public, gives voice to interests and principles whose locus is a public, serves as an instrument with which to test public truths and values and to select

---

manuscript of his *Lectures on Rhetoric and Belles Lettres* be destroyed upon his death. The lectures were finally published in 1963 following the discovery of a near-complete set of student lecture notes (taken during 1762-1763) in a manor-house auction in 1958.

and justify public means and ends. In general, rhetoric at its best sustains wisdom in the life of a public. (Bitzer 68).

Bitzer goes on to discuss rhetoric's long history of sustaining public wisdom, beginning in ancient Greece and continuing to the present day. Central to his argument is the idea that "the formation of the public requires community, and community requires the sharing of rich symbols, interests, and ideas" (Bitzer 80). Rhetoric also serves the creation of public knowledge by "sustain[ing] its experiential knowledge, providing modes of debate and discussion needed for intelligent decision and action" (Bitzer 80). Perhaps most importantly, in relation to the development of a novelistic horizon of expectation, Bitzer asserts that a "public that would maintain its identity will learn, rehearse, and celebrate what it knows; it will not only experience its personal facts, but also will display and sometimes dramatize them" (Bitzer 88). These intertwined concepts – that rhetoric creates and sustains public knowledge, and that public knowledge is rehearsed and dramatized by the public – explain both the centrality of rhetoric in creating horizons of expectation and the role of the novel in dramatizing public knowledge. The standard bearer for promoting and supporting public knowledge about taste and literary judgment through rhetoric at the close of the eighteenth century was Hugh Blair.

Hugh Blair and the Influence of Eighteenth-Century British Rhetoric

An examination of Hugh Blair's lectures is perhaps the best way to understand the cultural pervasiveness of belletristic rhetoric in novel theory and criticism at the turn of the eighteenth century. Blair's *Lectures on Rhetoric and Belles Lettres* demonstrate a marked shift away from the re-formulation of classical rhetorical theory that dominated the first half of the eighteenth century: while Patricia Bizzell and Bruce Herzberg observe that Blair's rhetoric is somewhat indebted to Quintilian in its civic-minded purpose (Bizzell and Herzberg 947), Linda Ferreira-Buckley and S. Michael Halloran maintain that in Blair "the focus of rhetoric shifted from the one who invents ... to the one who receives ... It shifted emphasis from a generative to an analytic art" (Ferreira-Buckley and Halloran xv). While Blair's rhetoric hardly ignores oratory or textual production – he devotes the majority of his lectures to the classical canons of arrangement, style, and delivery – his work is clearly intended to help the receiver, whether hearer or reader, develop an aesthetic sense of taste and judgment in composition. Ferreira-Buckley and Halloran characterize Blair's work as part of a movement – including the work of Lord Kames, Joshua Reynolds, and David Hume – toward "an aesthetic rhetoric" (Ferreira-Buckley and Halloran xlvii).

Blair begins to develop the importance of taste in his lectures in the preface, stating that he hopes his lectures will provide a "comprehensive view" (Blair 1) of how to cultivate taste and in his first lecture, Blair explicitly states the importance of taste in his rhetorical system: he acknowledges that while many readers of his lectures may be attempting to improve their oratorical or compositional abilities, "others . . . may wish only to improve their taste with respect to writing and discourse, and to acquire principles which will enable them to judge [literature] for themselves" (Blair 5). The development of taste and judgment is, then, a primary – if not *the* primary – concern of Blair's work.

But while taste is a central concern in Blair's rhetoric, it is by no means a simple concept. Blair does manage to succinctly define taste in Lecture II as "[t]he power of receiving pleasure from the beauties of nature and of art" (Blair 10). Yet even though Blair later states that "the application of reason and good sense to . . . productions of genius" (Blair 13) is one of the best ways to develop taste, taste depends far more on an individual's intuition than on powers of reason:

> Taste is not resolvable into any such operation of Reason. It is not merely through a discovery of the understanding, or a deduction of argument, that the mind receives pleasure from a . . . fine poem. Such objects often strike us intuitively, and make a strong impression, when we are unable to assign the reasons of being pleased. (Blair 10)

Blair not only sees taste as an intuitive response to objects of beauty: taste also occupies a primal space in the human mind. Blair contends that "[i]t is no less essential to man to have some discernment of beauty, than it is to possess the attributes of reason and speech" (Blair 11). Yet while Blair sees an intuitive sense of the beautiful as fundamentally human as the powers of speech and reason, Blair is quick to qualify this idea by noting a "remarkable inequality" (Blair 11) in the distribution of a sense of taste which can be truly refined.

Blair continues to refine his definition of taste, stating that taste is a "faculty [which] seems more nearly allied to a feeling of sense, than to a process of understanding" (Blair 10). He later delineates the various ways in which reason is necessary to the development of taste, but it is important to note that Blair's introductory remarks on taste see taste as a faculty, naturally occurring in all people, which is primarily a function of feeling, emotion, and intuition which reason only serves to refine and develop. This relation of taste to intuition and emotion also serves to ground true taste in moral development: Blair points out that there can be no true apprehension of beauty "without our possessing virtuous affections" and the lack of a proper moral sense results in an imperfect taste which has "a very imperfect relish of the highest beauties of eloquence and poetry" (Blair 14).

However, Blair gives little attention to how an individual might develop these necessary virtuous affections. He does provide some sense of how virtuous affections might develop in Lecture XXXIV, as Blair focuses on improving in eloquence through the development of moral sense. Blair clearly believes that an individual's moral sense is an inborn faculty that is perfected through concentrated effort: "[Nature] must sow the seeds; but culture is requisite for bringing these seeds to perfection" (Blair 380). The suggestion here is that moral sense, while present in all people, must be effectively trained to reach its full potential. The possession of a finely tuned moral sense, Blair asserts, is the most important quality to possess in developing effective oratory, and the foundation for establishing personal character is located in virtue (Blair 381-382). Blair does not recommend a specific course of action for developing virtue, but he does suggest that virtue and intellectual development are inextricably connected, claiming "[n]othing is so favourable as Virtue to the prosecution of honourable studies" (Blair 382). Blair outlines the characteristics of virtue that should be present in an effective rhetor: "love of justice and order . . . the love of honesty and truth . . . the love of liberty . . . zeal for all great and noble designs, and reverence for all worthy and heroic characters" (Blair 382). Most importantly, perhaps, is Blair's understanding of how the possession of these characteristics will impact a rhetor's interaction and identification with his audience:

> Joined with the manly virtues, he should, at the same time, possess strong and tender sensibility to all the injuries, distresses, and sorrows of his fellow-creatures; a heart that can easily relent; that can readily enter into the circumstances of others, and can make their case his own. (Blair 383)

The "strong and tender" sensibility described by Blair is remarkably novelistic in tone: J. Paul Hunter has argued that one of the primary characteristics of early British novels is a tendency to invite novel readers to vicariously participate in the narrative (Hunter 24). And while in this instance Blair is specifically addressing eloquence and oratory, throughout his lectures he makes it clear that the principles of oratorical composition can and should apply to any form of discourse: as he states in the Preface, the *Lectures* are intended to assist any individual who hopes to "cultivate their Taste, to form their Style, or to prepare themselves for Public Speaking or Composition" (Blair 1).

The emphasis on the development of moral sense accompanying the development of proper taste and judgment addresses many of the fears associated with novel reading at the end of the eighteenth century. Blair acknowledges that novels may not seem to warrant any serious attention but argues that "any kind of Writing . . . that obtains a general currency, and especially that early pre-occupies the imagination of the youth of both sexes, must demand particular attention. Its influence is likely to be considerable, both on the morals and taste of a nation" (Blair 420). Tellingly, Blair's project is conceived in relation to both individual readership and broad cultural formation. Blair's appreciation for the novel genre is firmly rooted in the eighteenth-century commonplace of linking fictional narratives to moral purpose, an approach that was to become familiar territory in the defense of the novel:

> [F]ictitious histories might be employed for very useful purposes. They furnish one of the best channels for conveying instruction, for painting human life and manners, for showing the errors into which we are betrayed by our passions, for rendering virtue amiable and vice odious. The effect of well-contrived stories . . . is stronger than any effect that can be produced by simple and naked instruction. (Blair 421)

Blair continues, defending the novel on a historical basis by claiming that "the wisest men in all ages have more or less employed fables and fictions as the vehicles of knowledge . . . It is not, therefore, the nature of this sort of Writing . . . but the faulty execution, that can expose it to any contempt" (Blair 421). Such a strong endorsement of a genre that was often viewed, in Blair's time, as morally suspect and potentially dangerous might seem bold for a conservative professor and Presbyterian minister like Blair, but his views about the novel's ability to infuse the reader with a proper moral sense were hardly unique or original.

Yet in Blair we find that the impulse to defend the novel on those grounds – moral purpose linked with aesthetic function – is firmly rooted in *belles lettres* rhetoric. Belletristic rhetorical theory and training met the need for readers to develop proper taste and judgment to read novels critically; in the nineteenth century, critics, reviewers, and readers of novels consistently evaluated novels based a text's ability to fuse ethics and aesthetics. Blair's significance in developing a novel-reading horizon of expectation does not, then, lie in the originality of his thought – as Michael McKeon and others have observed, the intertwined relationship of literature and didactic purpose was well-established and widely affirmed throughout the eighteenth century (McKeon 600). The importance of Blair and his *Lectures on Rhetoric and Belles Lettres* is found, instead, in the extent of his influence.

Blair began his lecture series at the University of Edinburgh in 1759, and the lectures were first published in 1783. However, tracking the publication and distribution of texts during the eighteenth and nineteenth centuries is a difficult task. In the case of a text as popular as Blair's *Lectures*, which was widely anthologized in textbooks and collections of unofficial "extracts," establishing exact numbers for publication or readership is almost impossible. But the significance of the lectures is hard to overestimate. Miller asserts that upon their publication in 1783, "Blair's *Lectures on Rhetoric and Belles Lettres* swept the emerging field [of English studies], passing through over one hundred and ten editions" (Miller 2). James L. Golden and Edward P.J. Corbett are more specific: "The *Lectures* had a phenomenal sale . . . during the first century after publication . . . Robert M. Schmitz list[s] twenty-six editions in Great Britain . . . and fifty-two abridged editions" (Golden and Corbett 25). In their 2005 introduction to Blair's *Lectures*, Linda Ferreira-Buckley and S. Michael Halloran argue that Blair's works were among the most influential English studies texts of the latter eighteenth century and the first half of the nineteenth (Ferreira-Buckley and

Halloran xv-xxiii). Ferreira-Buckley and Halloran also observe that Blair's influence extended beyond the classroom to informal study in book groups, home study, and mechanics institutes. This study outside of a university classroom setting was, significantly, focused on correct reading and interpretation:

> It was necessary to read widely, but reading alone did not constitute education, for it was necessary to assess that reading—to understand its merits and demerits, both linguistically and morally; the linguistic dimension was presumed to be a window into the moral value of a text. Blair's *Lectures* helped one learn such discrimination. (Ferreira-Buckley and Halloran xxii)

As Ferriera-Buckley and Halloran argue, Blair's influence penetrated every stratum of literate British culture. Ferreira-Buckley and Halloran go on to acknowledge that Blair's rhetoric was not "an emancipatory rhetoric but one complicit with dominant ideologies," yet the *Lectures* found application within an incredibly wide range of political and social ideologies. Bizzell and Herzberg in turn describe Blair as "the Quintilian of his time, combining in his rhetoric a theory that met with nearly universal approval and a pedagogy that won nearly universal application" (Bizzell and Herzberg 947). Among historians of rhetoric, then, there is no doubt about the influence and importance of Blair – and through Blair, eighteenth-century rhetorical theory – in the development of literary criticism in the nineteenth century.

There are criticisms of Blair, primarily focused on his lack of originality, which are perfectly legitimate. However, I do not argue for the originality of Blair's thinking or for *belles lettres* as the only articulation of the philosophical and epistemological theories that were brought to bear on the questions of literacy, morality, and the novel during this period. What I am arguing for is a reassessment of the influence of belletristic rhetorical theory in shaping those questions and the attendant responses.

Influence, though, is incredibly difficult to ascertain. As William St. Clair observes in *The Reading Nation in the Romantic Period*, "[h]ow to assess influence is among the most difficult of all the methodological challenges that historians face in attempting to understand the diffusionary rise and fall of ideas" (St. Clair 268). Despite this difficulty, St. Clair asserts that Blair's *Lectures on Rhetoric and Belles Lettres* can be taken, with Burke's *Philosophical Enquiry in the Sublime and Beautiful*, as the most widely read and accepted aesthetic statements of the eighteenth century (St. Clair 270; 581; 583). But St. Clair's exhaustive appendices reveal the comparative distribution of Blair's *Lectures* versus Burke's *Enquiry* was hardly equal. Between 1783 and 1825, 20,500 copies of Blair's *Lectures on Rhetoric and Belles Lettres* were printed. Furthermore, St. Clair's account of the print runs for Blair does not include the immense profusion of texts that made use of Blair's rhetoric in extracts, anthologies, and unacknowledged printings.

By comparison, only 4,000 copies of Burke's *Enquiry* are known to have been published between 1757 and 1807[7].

St. Clair also argues that Blair's *Sermons*, first published in 1778, are the most useful text for identifying an "official ideology" during the romantic period (St. Clair 270). The *Sermons* were "officially recommended as a source from which all those in authority could safely draw in giving their own advice" (St. Clair 270), and the archival records show that almost a quarter of a million copies of Blair's *Sermons* were sold by 1815 (St. Clair 271). The *Lectures on Rhetoric and Belles Lettres* were endorsed as enthusiastically as his *Sermons* and sold very well in their own right. St. Clair demonstrates that versions of Blair's *Sermons* and *Lectures*, in extracts and anthologies, were used across a broad spectrum of the reading public throughout the romantic period and beyond (St. Clair 280).

Blair has been justifiably criticized for a lack of originality, and his rhetoric has been described as primarily managerial in its presentation and synthesis of widely known and commonly accepted conceptions of developing, delivering, and understanding discourse of all kinds. Duncan Wu, for example, cites a letter in which W.B.J. Owen scoffs at Blair for "spouting the commonplaces of the age" (qtd. in Wu 24). But Blair's ability to synthesize and systematize the wide range of eighteenth-century influences found in the *Lectures* is precisely the quality that made his work so widely praised. St. Clair argues just this point: "Blair's weakness was the essence of the appeal. It was because he replayed the commonplaces and *senttentiae* of the culture of his day that he was, and is, so useful" (St. Clair 273). The accessibility and familiarity of Blair's work allowed it to permeate British culture of the romantic period, influencing the development of literary criticism and readerly expectations throughout the next century. Blair's insistence on the belletristic fusion of moral sense with aesthetic purpose provided the basis of criticism of the novel well into the latter half of the nineteenth century.

Thus, the wide extent of Blair's influence certainly reveals rhetoric's crucial role in creating the horizon of expectation for novel readers at the end of the eighteenth century. Blair's establishment of an aesthetic rooted in propriety, probability, and moral purpose helped ensconce those elements as the basis for developing correct critical judgments about novels. Claiming that the eighteenth-century novel reading public's horizon of expectation focused on propriety, probability, and morality is hardly an original argument, but asserting that Hugh Blair – and belletristic rhetorical concepts – became part of what Jauss

---

[7] St. Clair's appendices acknowledge that there were at several print runs of unknown quantity of Burke's *Enquiry* during these years. But of the known quantities, no edition of the *Enquiries* seems to have been printed in larger numbers than 1,500 at a time and many printings only numbered 500.

refers to as "a semiotic system that accomplishes itself between the development and the correction of a system" (Jauss 167) is perhaps more bold. *Belles lettres* rhetoric is a key component in understanding how readers at the end of the eighteenth century approached novels, providing a foundation for conceptualizing a "horizon of expectation and rules familiar from earlier texts, which are then varied, corrected, altered, or even just reproduced" (Jauss 167). Looking ahead to the novel histories, theories, and canons that developed during the Romantic era, we will see how often the expectations and rules carried over from earlier texts were varied or altered and how often those expectations were simply reproduced.

Chapter 5
"Let me make the novels:" *Belles Lettres* Rhetoric and Novel Criticism in the Romantic Era

> *I propose to trace Romance to its Origin, to follow its progress through the different periods to its declension, to shew how the modern Novel sprung up out of its ruins, to examine and compare the merits of both, and to remark upon the effects of them.*
>
> Clara Reeve, *The Progress of Romance*

In 1704, Scottish politician and patriot Andrew Fletcher famously stated his belief that "if a Man were permitted to make all the ballads, he should not care who should make the laws of a nation" (Fletcher 10). Fletcher's maxim rests on the cultural power and pervasiveness of ballads within the Scottish literary tradition: the ballad tradition was held in such high regard by a broad cross-section of the Scottish population that Fletcher implies that the ballad-makers had at least as much influence as the lawmakers. When Hugh Blair addressed the cultural value and merit of novels in Lecture XXXVII of his *Lectures on Rhetoric and Belles Lettres* in 1783[1], he turned to Fletcher to help him explain the ever-growing power and influence of the genre:

> There remains . . . a very insignificant class of Writings, known by the name of Romances and Novels. These may, at first view, seem too insignificant, to deserve that any particular notice should be taken of them. But I cannot be of this opinion. Mr. Fletcher of Salton . . . quotes it as the saying of a wise man, that give him the making of all the ballads of a nation, he would allow any one that pleased to make their laws. The saying . . . is applicable to the subject now before us. (Blair 420)

---

[1] Blair began his lecture series on rhetoric and *belles lettres* at the University of Edinburgh in 1759, and only published the lectures in 1783. His lecture notes from 1779 indicate that this line of thought concerning novels and their influence was present in his work prior to the formal publication of the *Lectures*.

The subject before Blair in Lecture XXXVII is a relatively brief discussion of the history, nature, and canon of British novels. Blair uses Fletcher to deflect criticism: novels may *seem* trifling, Blair tells us, but their influence cannot be denied.

Decades later, in 1810, Anna Laetitia Barbauld also paraphrased Fletcher – or perhaps Blair – in her introduction to *The British Novelists*, a fifty-volume anthology of twenty-nine titles from twenty-two novelists. Like Blair, Barbauld's assessment of the genre begins with a history of the genre with its roots in antiquity, and while her recitation of the history of the novel clearly borrows from Clara Reeve, John Moore, James Beattie, and others (Johnson 167), the introduction finishes with a remarkable flourish. Barbauld concludes the introduction with a nod to Fletcher, proclaiming, "[l]et me make the novels of a country, and let who will make the systems" (Barbauld 59). After proclaiming the power of novels to shape national character, Barbauld proceeds to develop her canon[2] – to "make" the novels of England – at the outset of the nineteenth century.

Barbauld's critical essay on the character and history of novels was, and continues to be, one of the most important early critical assessments of the genre in English. Claudia Johnson claims that "her [Barbauld's] *The British Novelists* constitutes the first novelistic canon" (Johnson 166), and as such, the prefatory essay deserves a great deal of attention. Along the way, however, Johnson observes that Barbauld certainly referenced prior histories of the genre, citing Richard Hurd, James Beattie, Thomas Warton, Clara Reeve, and John Moore as likely influences[3] (Johnson 167). Clearly, Barbauld's 1810 history of the novel was not alone at the time: during the years between 1760 and 1820, the British novel as a genre underwent a significant and extensive critical assessment. Joseph Bunn Heidler, in his 1928 study *The History, from 1700 to 1800, of English Criticism of Prose Fiction*, cites sixty-seven different texts published between 1760 and 1800 alone which critically address the novel (Heidler 172 – 176). Although Heidler includes many works that are not primarily critical in their purpose – including biographical notes, prefaces, and the texts of novels themselves – he creates an extensive chronological bibliography of eighteenth-century novel criticism. Some of these references are no longer than a paragraph or two; others are multi-volume works such as Lord Kames' *Elements of Criticism* or Clara Reeve's

---

[2] Blair also developed a novel canon of sorts after referencing Fletcher. Blair's list of profitable and useful novels includes works by le Sage, Marivaux, Rousseau, Defoe, Fielding, and Richardson.

[3] Noticeably absent from Johnson's list of influences on Barbauld, of course, is Hugh Blair, from whom it seems likely Barbauld borrowed the paraphrase of Andrew Fletcher.

The Progress of Romance. And though Heidler's work is not exhaustive, it does serve to underscore the extent to which the novel was theorized in the late eighteenth century. Heidler's list includes familiar names like Laurence Sterne, Oliver Goldsmith, Jean-Jacques Rousseau, Horace Walpole, Tobias Smollett, Fanny Burney, William Cowper, James Beattie, Clara Reeve, and William Godwin, as well as lesser lights. For example, Clara Reeve's now well-known *Progress of Romance* is present, but so are unfamiliar and mostly forgotten works like Thomas James Mathias' satirical poem, *The Pursuits of Literature*, first published in 1794 (Heidler 176).

It seems worthwhile, then, to examine the reasons why histories and critical assessments of the novel took hold during the Romantic[4] era. As discussed in the previous chapter, there was a great deal of concern in the late eighteenth and early nineteenth century about the swift democratization of the reading public and novels were at the center such concerns. Richard Altick observes in *The English Common Reader* that the "popularity [of novels] touched off the first widespread discussion of the social effects of a democratized reading audience" (Altick 63). Critics and intellectuals, clerics and politicians all sounded off about the merits or dangers of the novel. As previously noted, Hugh Blair – a critic, intellectual, and cleric – defends his discussion of novels by arguing that "any kind of Writing, how trifling soever in appearance, that obtains a general currency, and especially that early pre-occupies the imagination of the youth of both sexes, must demand particular attention. Its influence is likely to be considerable, both on the morals and taste of a nation" (Blair 420–421). William St. Clair characterizes Blair's attitude as typical: "[w]hen literature elevated feelings of readers, many believed, it could help to sustain religious and moral values. But when it conferred an apparent legitimacy on ideas, emotions, and types of behaviour which readers had not previously seen articulated and fixed in print, it became dangerously unsettling" (St. Clair 12–13). Because the novel was perceived as – and in many cases, actually was – the preferred reading material of the newly literate classes, the genre naturally came under a great deal of scrutiny.

---

[4] I use the term "romantic" with some hesitation. The idea of romanticism is, perhaps, an over-determined concept, and in this instance I am using it very specifically to denote the years between 1780 and 1820 or so, and not as a description of the novel criticism of the period. British Romanticism (especially as developed by Wordsworth and Coleridge) certainly owes a great deal to classical and belletristic rhetorical theory, as Walter Jackson Bate thoroughly demonstrates in *From Classic to Romantic: Premises of Taste in Eighteenth Century England*. Nevertheless, I do not mean to imply that the novel criticism of the romantic period was necessarily what might be considered romantic in nature.

One of the results of this critical scrutiny was the production of a large number of critical histories of the genre that invariably included a list of titles that were intended to be regarded as canonical by their eighteenth-century readers. Yet the current critical consensus (if such a thing ever exists) seems confident that there was no established canon until Barbauld's groundbreaking 1810 essay. Claudia Johnson says as much when she claims that Barbauld's canon was the first, and other critics agree, if for other reasons. In *The Rise of the Novel*, which Johnson derides for relying upon the now-orthodox triumvirate of Defoe, Richardson, and Fielding, Ian Watt claims that not only was there no commonly agreed upon canon, the very idea of what constituted a novel was in question until the end of the eighteenth century (Watt 10). William St. Clair, in his wide-ranging examination of Romantic era readership and literacy, admits that if there was, in fact, a canon of British fiction at the end of the eighteenth century, it was a "direct result" of the 1774 legal decision concerning copyright law in Britain and the resultant mad scramble by publishers and booksellers to take advantage of newly available titles before the copyright window closed once again (St. Clair 132).[5] Yet St. Clair observes that while the 1774 decision may have made canonization possible in the publication industry, the fiction canon at the end of the eighteenth century "is not wholly explainable as an economic response to an economic opportunity" (St. Clair 132). Of course, very few historical phenomena are explainable as the result of a single event. In the case of the novel canon at the outset of the nineteenth century, there are any number of social, political, and economic factors that come to bear on any assessment of such a canon. Through a close examination of six Romantic-era studies of the novel, this chapter will describe and investigate just one of those factors: the clear influence of belletristic rhetorical theory on the critics who historicized, theorized, and canonized the British novel as the eighteenth century drew to a close and the nineteenth century began.

The sustained critical evaluation of the novel at this time produced, primarily, three different but interrelated assessments: histories of the novel, theories of the novel, and canons of the novel. Quite often, all three appear in the

---

[5] St. Clair's explanation of the far-reaching ramifications of the 1774 decision is lucid, though complex. In brief, St. Clair convincingly argues that perpetual copyright, which was struck down – temporarily – in 1774, "prevented formal canonizing ... Before 1774, a proposal to publish such a series, from, say Chaucer to Thomson, would have involved research among the records of the Stationer's Company, publishers' wills, and the book trade's closed sales catalogues, to find all the current shareholders of the much divided intellectual properties and then persuading them to engage in a jointly financed enterprise, and the idea seems never even to have been contemplated" (St. Clair 123).

same text. In this chapter I will closely examine the novel histories, theories, and canons developed by James Beattie, Clara Reeve, John Moore, Anna Lætitia Barbauld, John Colin Dunlop, and Walter Scott,[6] primarily highlighting the presence of existing belletristic critical concepts in the development of novel histories, theories, and canons of the Romantic era.

The studies selected for examination in this chapter were chosen based on a few important criteria. First, all the selected texts address the history of the novel, examine the nature and purpose of the novel, and posit a canon of British novels.[7] Second, the selected texts frequently reference and interact with each other, demonstrating awareness of an ongoing contemporary critical examination of the novel and indicating the clear presence of a novel reading horizon of expectation. Finally, and perhaps most importantly, the texts were selected for the variety of contexts in which they were written. William St. Clair argues that the canonization and theorization of the novel during the Romantic era was primarily a product of economic necessity and copyright legality (St. Clair 122–130). As Claudia Johnson observes, this is certainly the context in which Barbauld and Scott produced their novel histories and theories, though neither author's editorial selections were based entirely on economic considerations (Johnson 168; 173). The argument for the economic and copyright factors, however, only makes sense for critics who, like Barbauld and Scott, were making editorial decisions for publishing collections of novels. Other critics, such as Beattie and Reeve, theorized the novel in a more abstract setting; that is, their conceptualizations of the novel were not directly tied to such specific economic or legal considerations. Reeve's *Progress of Romance*, for example, was not published as prefatory material for any anthologies or editions: Reeve's work was published "for the author by W. Keymer" (Reeve, front matter to *The Progress of Romance*) and lasted for only one edition. The authors of the selected critical texts represent a wide range of backgrounds: there are novelists and poets, critics and rhetoricians, clergy and scholars, high church and low, men and women. There is one point of consistency, however: all the authors represent the upper-middle class. As Thomas Miller observes, the desire to theorize and systematize

---

[6] The texts are presented in chronological order: Beattie's *On Fable and Romance* (1783), Reeve's *Progress of Romance* (1785), Moore's *A View of the Commencement and Progress of Romance* (1797), Barbauld's "On the Origin and Progress of Novel Writing" (1810), Dunlop's *The History of Fiction* (1814/1845), Scott's *Notices Biographical and Critical* (1820/1829) and "Essay on Romance" (1824).

[7] When I claim that each author posits a canon of British novels, I do not mean that each author explicitly offers a list of canonical titles. But each author does choose novels, judging them acceptable or unacceptable on a clear set of criteria. Judging and choosing literature based on accepted standards of good taste is, of course, a belletristic activity.

British language and literature – including the novel – was an outgrowth of a collective attempt to shape the culture in which the middle class found themselves to have increasing influence, a desire that is essentially belletristic in its outlook and design (Miller 13; 146–147).

The History of the Novel in the Romantic Era

Any discussion of the history of the novel as understood during the Romantic era is difficult for a number of reasons, not the least of which is the terminology of such histories. In Romantic-era accounts of the genre, the history of the novel is consistently developed in relationship to prior genres, with the epic and romance traditions the most prominent. But other genres play a role: "eastern tales" are frequently discussed and alluded to, as are "true histories[8]." Many of these novel histories include extensive accounts of western European history, focusing closely on medieval social and political structures as foundational to the development of historically-based romance traditions (Beattie 28; Reeve 14–16; Moore v–xxxi; Barbauld 8–12; Dunlop 55–185; Scott, "Essay on Romance" 65–106). While all these accounts of romance, epic, history, and chivalry demonstrate a remarkable level of congruence, such accounts also muddy the waters through the use of so many different terms to discuss the development of prose fiction. Clara Reeve addresses this problem early in *The Progress of Romance* when, in the character of novel- and romance-defender Euphrasia, she responds to her interlocutors' superficial concerns over semantics:

> Let me bespeak your favour, by assuring you that I mean to do something more than merely to investigate *names*: we will afterwards proceed to consider the beauties and defects of these writings, of the uses and abuses, and of their effects upon the manners of the times in which they were written. I propose to trace Romance to its Origin, to follow its progress through the different periods to its declension, to shew how the modern Novel sprung up out of its ruins, to examine and compare the merits of both, and to remark upon the effects of them. (Reeve 8)

At issue for Reeve and the other critics gathered here is the development of prose fiction in Europe, from ancient times to the present. All of these critics agree that the prose fiction of the prior (eighteenth) century presented a sharp

---

[8] Everett Zimmerman argues that the association of prose fiction with historical accounts during the eighteenth century was due – at least in part – to the "commitment [of eighteenth-century novelists] to the historical as a relevant category for understanding their fictional achievements" (Zimmerman 1).

departure from the prose fiction that came before; not at issue is the question of terminology for this relatively new manifestation of fictional prose narratives that came to be known as the novel.

One area of uniformity in the histories of the novel presented by Beattie, Reeve, Moore, Barbauld, Dunlop, and Scott concerns the novel's roots in the epic and romance traditions. Beattie begins by arguing for the presence of didactic fictional narratives in all cultures beginning in ancient times. Beattie ascribes the popularity of fiction, at all periods in history, to "the weakness of human nature" and the inability of humanity to rely entirely upon reason and logic in the comprehension of truth (Beattie 1). Didactic fiction – from ancient fables to eighteenth-century novels – are compared to medicine for the weak of mind: "if a rude multitude cannot readily comprehend a moral or political doctrine . . . it may be as allowable to illustrate that doctrine by a fable . . . as it is for a physician to strengthen a weak stomach with cordials" (2). Reeve uses the same starting point as Beattie, crediting Beattie with "walk[ing] over the ground, and mark[ing] out [the] boundaries" of the history of the novel (Reeve viii). However, Reeve's conception of ancient fiction is based on entertainment as well as education: "Romances or Heroic fables are of very ancient, and I might say universal Origin. We find traces of them in all times, and in all countries: they have always been the favourite entertainment of the most savage, as well as the most civilized people" (Reeve 13–14). John Moore's account of ancient fiction begins with the Roman conquest: "as a *consolation* for the loss of liberty, the Romans communicated their arts, sciences, language, and manners, to their new subjects" (Moore vi). From this point, Moore proceeds to deliver a medieval history of Europe, speculating in the end that the more fantastical elements of the romance tradition might be attributed to Norse invasions or Middle Eastern influences via the Crusades (vi–xxviii). For Barbauld, the novel has its roots in ancient Greece and the near east, and then in a romance tradition fueled by Arthurian pseudo-history and chivalric tales propagated by French troubadours (Barbauld 3–12). John Colin Dunlop devotes the majority of his massive critical work to ancient and medieval antecedents of the British novel (13–185). Dunlop seems to almost paraphrase Reeve when he proclaims the breadth of prose fiction's reach across cultures and nations, asserting "fiction has in all ages formed the delight of the rudest and the most polished nations" (Dunlop 13). Scott places the origin of fictional narratives alongside the origin of historical narratives, arguing that "romance and real history have the same common origin . . . and [ancient and medieval histories] may be termed either romantic histories, or historical romances, according to the proportion in which their truth is debased by fiction, or their fiction mingled with truth" (Scott 67).

All these accounts of the novel's origins begin with ancient texts, typically the *Milesian Tales* or the *Golden Ass* of Apuleius. Frequent additions to the ancient fiction canon include *Theagenes and Chariclea* and Aesop's fables. Importantly, these Romantic-era critics were not attempting to blur the line between romance and the novel, and it is reasonable to assume that they would disagree with Margaret Anne Doody, who obliterates the line between romance and novel by her own declaration that such distinctions have been used "disingenuously" and that such distinctions have "often done more harm than good" (Doody 16). But the distinction between romance and the novel is central to these Romantic-era histories of the genre. Unlike Doody, however, whose intention is to recover and demonstrate the novel's feminist and multi-cultural genealogy, the Romantic-era critics develop their history around a belletristic attempt to emphasize prose fiction's respectable lineage.

The emphasis on a respectable literary heritage is crucial to *belles lettres* critical ventures. This is because the twin concepts of taste and judgment are central to *belles lettres* criticism (Warnick 95–127), and the best way to develop correct taste and judgment is to spend time in the presence of works that were widely acclaimed for their proper aesthetic values. Blair argues that the only way to develop proper taste for the aesthetics of written discourse is through "attention to the most approved models, study of the best authors, [and] comparisons of lower and higher degrees of the same beauties" (Blair 12). Additionally, sound judgment only develops through the continued exercise of correct taste, which includes not only sound reason and aesthetic appreciation, but also moral rectitude (Blair 13), a concept to which I will return later in this chapter. One of the reasons the novel was a suspect genre throughout the eighteenth century was precisely because it lacked a literary pedigree that allowed readers to develop correct taste and judgment. Blair advocates "attention to the most approved models, study of the best authors, [and] comparisons of lower and higher degrees of the same beauties" (Blair 12). Yet until the novel canon began to form at the end of the eighteenth century, there was no agreement upon the approved models and best authors, and thus no basis for comparing the relative merits of different novels.

At stake in these novel histories, in other words, is the genre's suitability for inclusion as a respectable genre, worthy to stand with poetry, drama, history, and the epic as deserving critical attention and respect. These histories of the novel attempted to answer this question by developing a literary pedigree that would establish the novel as a genre well within the acceptable standards of taste. This idea is most clearly on display in Reeve's *The Progress of*

Romance. In the preface, Reeve states that her intention for *The Progress of Romance* is "to assist according to my best judgment, the reader's choice, amidst the almost infinite variety it affords, in a selection of such are most worthy of a place in the libraries of readers of every class" (Reeve iv). Reeve closes the preface with her declaration that, with the proper development of taste and judgment, novels and romances will be shown to be "equally entitled to our attention and respect, as any other works of Genius and literature" (Reeve xvi). Blair describes the relationship between taste and genius as the difference between the ability to judge and the ability to execute (Blair 23). Thus in belletristic rhetoric, genius indicates the ability to attain the highest level of achievement in any field of human endeavor. Reeve repeatedly invokes genius as one of her criteria for judging prose fiction (Reeve, Vol. I 7–9; 21; 25; 32; 97; Vol. II 40; 41; 77; 80; 96), which allows her to argue for the aesthetic achievement of great prose fiction, no matter what such fiction is labeled. [9]

The body of Reeve's *The Progress of Romance* begins with a sustained and rigorous attempt to link prose fiction – both romances and novels[10] – to the approved and respectable epic tradition. Reeve clearly has no intention of defending all prose fiction; instead, using belletristic language, she explains that her defense of romance and the novel will "remark upon the most eminent works of the kind, and . . . pay the tribute of praise to works of Genius and morality" (Reeve Vol. I 9). In her defense of prose fiction, Reeve defines romance as "heroic fable" or, in a Fielding-esque turn of phrase, "Epic in prose" (Reeve Vol. I 13). As Reeve proceeds through the second dialogue, she links another belletristic concept – probability – to the development of prose fiction, and in the process associates romance and novel with history and epic: "[a]s a country became civilized, their narrations were methodized, and moderated to probability" (Reeve Vol. I 14). By the end of the second dialogue, Reeve establishes the two criteria upon which she bases her entire defense of prose fiction: "First, that Epic Poetry is the parent of Romance. Secondly, that there is a certain degree of respect due to all the works of Genius, by whatever name distinguished" (Reeve Vol. I 25). Reeve goes on to demonstrate the relationship between

---

[9] Beattie, Moore, Barbauld, Dunlop, and Scott all mention genius as a component in selecting texts for inclusion, a topic to which I will return later in this chapter.

[10] Reeve repeatedly maintains the distinction between romances and novels, though she understands the genres to exist in close relationship with one another.

romances and novels, thus establishing the epic as the suitably respectable literary forebear for novels.

To some degree, all the novel histories studied here attempt to create a credible literary pedigree for the novel. Trevor Ross argues that eighteenth-century canon formation depended upon such attempts at genre-historicization as "a consensual harmony was recast as the verdict of history, conceived either retrospectively as a 'test of time' or prospectively as a distant point in futurity" (Ross 92). This concept is evident throughout the novel studies presented in this chapter: James Beattie bases his historical argument on the necessity of fiction in communicating and teaching the masses. John Moore works to show his readers that fiction has been intricately woven into the fiber of western culture and history for centuries, while Barbauld is more blunt: a great novel is simply the venerable epic recast in prose (Barbauld 3). John Colin Dunlop, in the most objectionably Euro- and Anglo-centric novel history of the six, cites the "indolent and voluptuous nations of the East" (Dunlop 13) as the birthplace of fictional prose narratives. As such, prose fiction is merely tolerable, but (as the balance of Dunlop's work goes on to argue) after fiction came into contact with the influence of western Europe, the genre was refined and made acceptable for the taste of British sensibilities. And finally, Scott draws a clear line of descent, from the excellencies of the ancient and medieval romances, through the "most tedious and dull" (Scott 107) romances of the seventeenth century, to a conclusion in the modern romance of the eighteenth century, in which "De Foe [sic] rendered fiction more impressive than truth itself" (Scott 108).

The close examination of these novel histories shows us that efforts to develop histories of the novel during the romantic era often took on belletristic overtones. The appeal to historically respectable genres reflects a belletristic interest in establishing the novel as part of a larger tradition of literary excellence and the repeated appeals to taste and genius as historical hallmarks of excellence in literary – and especially, prose fictional – discourse are central to the *belles lettres* approach to developing correct judgment in readers. But Beattie, Reeve, and the rest did more than simply provide an acceptable historical context for understanding prose fiction: each of the six also theorized about the nature, purpose, and function of the novel. And as with Congreve a century earlier, *belles lettres* provided the critical framework and terminology for theorizing the novel in the Romantic era.

The Theory of the Novel in the Romantic Era

Congreve's definition of the novel in 1692's *Incognita* underwent remarkably little change in the following century. Congreve's definition is succinct and to the point:

> Novels are of a more familiar Nature; Come near us, and represent to us Intrigues in practice, delight us with Accidents and odd Events, but not such as are wholly unusual or unpresidented [sic], such which not being so distant from our Belief bring also the pleasure nearer us. Romances give more Wonder, Novels more Delight. (preface to *Incognita*)

As already observed in Chapter 2, Samuel Johnson's 1751 essay on the novel in the *Rambler*, no. 4 explains the modern romance in very similar terms:

> The works of fiction, with which the present generation seems more particularly delighted, exhibit life in its true state, diversified only by accidents that happen daily in the world, and influenced by passions and qualities which are really to be found in conversing with mankind . . . [i]ts province is to bring about natural events by easy means, and to keep up curiosity without the help of wonder. (Johnson, The Rambler 18)

And at the end of the century, definitions of the novel still adhered to a very similar set of criteria: the novel is understood to be different from prior prose fiction in its attention to the common and everyday, its interest in the particular and individual, and its rejection of supernatural and marvelous plot elements. The belletristic critical concepts of verisimilitude, probability, and propriety are found in conjunction with a belletristic concern for morality, taste, and genius. The *belles lettres* horizon of expectation articulated in Blair's *Lectures* is present throughout the theories of the novel presented by Beattie, Reeve, Moore, Barbauld, Dunlop, and Scott.

Theory, of course, is another over-determined concept. Most of the texts under examination here hardly exhibit a purposefully cohesive or consistent theory of the novel. But they do theorize *about* the novel. The genre is described and evaluated based on clearly stated criteria, most of which are derived from belletristic principles. Such theorization is informal and not intended, in most cases, to be taken as a systematic theory. Individually, these texts offer what seem to be the private musings of thoughtful, well-read novel readers and writers of the Romantic era. But taken as a whole, these six texts offer a surprisingly cohesive analysis of the novel genre. The most striking examples of congruence among these theories of the novel occur in three areas: the definition of the novel in opposition to earlier prose romances, the definition of the novel in relation to the realistic and commonplace (as opposed to the supernatural and marvelous), and the utility of the novel in inculcating virtue and morality.

One of the most obvious features of these theories of the novel is a uniform understanding of the novel in opposition to the romance. Significantly, each of these critics – save Beattie – make reference to the novel as a genre unto itself, and the term "novel" is variously associated with the idea of a "new" or "modern" romance. Reeve is perhaps the most blunt about the divide she sees between novels and romances: while she allows that the two genres are frequently misunderstood as indistinguishable from one another, she asserts that "[n]o writings are more different than the ancient *Romance* and the modern *Novel*" (Reeve 7). Barbauld also draws a distinction between the novel and romance, though her description of it is much less pronounced. Barbauld describes the progress of the romance tradition from ancient Greece to the seventeenth century and then simply announces that the first examples of a new species of prose fiction in English – the novel – came about within the last century in the work of Manley, Behn, and Haywood (Barbauld 34–35). Scott's conception of the separation between romance and the novel is more nuanced. Scott cites Samuel Johnson's definitions of romance and the novel, informing the reader that Johnson defines the romance as based upon "marvelous and uncommon" events. Johnson's conception of the novel, on the other hand, sees it as a simple tale with love as its central concern (Scott, "Essay on Romance" 65). Scott revises Johnson's definition of the novel (while tacitly agreeing to Johnson's definition of the romance) to focus on the novel's separation from the romance tradition. Scott understands the novel to be "a fictitious narrative, differing from the romance, because the events are accommodated to the ordinary train of human events, and the modern state of society" (Scott, "Essay on Romance" 65). Scott admits, though, that such a definition does not necessarily prevent prose fiction from containing elements of both genres.

The conception of the novel in opposition to the romance tradition almost always springs from one source: Cervantes' *Don Quixote*. In "On the Origin and Progress of Novel Writing," Barbauld clearly sees *Don Quixote* as the end of the romance tradition. Barbauld states that Cervantes "drove [medieval romances] off the field, and they have never since been able to rally their forces" (Barbauld 12). Barbauld's statement, though, echoes earlier claims about Cervantes. In 1783[11], James Beattie credits Cervantes with bringing about a large-scale change in European literature: "*The History of Don Quixote* . . . brought about a great revolution in the manners and

---

[11] Also in 1783, Blair argues that Cervantes' work did a great deal to "explode" the popularity of the romance tradition (Blair 422).

literature of Europe, by banishing the wild dreams of chivalry, and reviving a taste for the simplicity of nature" (Beattie 94). Beattie goes on to assert that Cervantes brought a definite end to romance, arguing "*Don Quixote* occasioned the death of the old romance, and gave birth to the new" (Beattie 96). Like Barbauld nearly three decades later, Beattie has no doubts about the effectiveness of *Don Quixote* in eradicating the romance tradition: the publication of Don Quixote, Beattie claims, caused chivalric romance literature to vanish, "as snow melts before the sun" (Beattie 95).

Beattie's and Barbauld's assessments are certainly over-confident about *Don Quixote*'s power, and romances obviously continued to be written and read long after Cervantes. But identifying *Don Quixote* as a turning point in the development of prose fiction is a common feature of Romantic era novel theory. Clara Reeve, for example, claims that Cervantes checked the popularity of chivalric romances, yet not so completely as was perhaps commonly assumed: "*Cervantes*... who by ridiculing Romance and Knight Errantry in his *Don Quixote*, in some degree checked this frenzy: but the effect of his ridicule was not so universal as is generally believed" (Reeve, Vol. I 58). John Moore echoes both Beattie and Reeve when he describes Cervantes' intent "to turn into ridicule the prevailing taste of his countrymen for writings filled with marvelous and unnatural adventures that never had existed but in books of chivalry" (Moore lxxxi). Moore goes on to credit Cervantes with demonstrating the power of prose fiction to realistically portray the details of day-to-day life: "he gave... the most convincing proof that the passions could be affected, the understanding instructed, mirth excited, and all the purposes of writing attained, by representations of real domestic life, without offending the modesty of nature" (lxxx). Dunlop writes that Cervantes composed *Don Quixote* "at a time when the spirit of practical knight errantry was extinguished, but the rage for the perusal of chivalrous extravagance continued unabated" (Dunlop 309). Cervantes' satire targeted "the folly of those... [who were] engrossed with the fabrication or perusal of romantic compositions" (Dunlop 309).

Scott also sees Cervantes as foundational, but for slightly different reasons than Beattie, Reeve, Moore, Barbauld, and Dunlop. To Scott, Cervantes' satire provides evidence that the romance tradition, while changing, was alive and well in the seventeenth century: "Even in the time of Cervantes, the Pastoral Romance... was prevailing to such an extent as made it worthy of his satire" (Scott, "Essay on Romance" 106). Scott goes on to blame the downfall of romance, not directly on Cervantes, but on the qualities of seventeenth-century romances that made them such an easy target for Cervantes. These romances, Scott tells the reader, were "with few exceptions the most dull and tedious species of composition that ever obtained temporary popularity" (Scott,

"Essay on Romance" 107). Romance, in other words, caused its own downfall as literary taste shifted and began to value realism and probability over marvelous and improbable plots.

The novel's separation from romance is almost always linked to the second common feature of romantic-era novel criticism: the novel as a realistic fictional prose account of the everyday and commonplace. Over and over, the critics presented here inform their readers that the horizon of expectation for prose fiction changed during the sixteenth and seventeenth centuries. Readers ceased to marvel over the fantastical tendencies of the romance tradition: in Blair's words, romances died out because "there was too much of the marvellous [sic] in them to please an age which now aspired to refinement" (Blair 423). In leaving behind the marvelous, prose fiction turned toward a belletristic embrace of probability and realism.

By the end of the seventeenth century, prose fiction had gradually, in James Beattie's words, "divested herself of her gigantic size, tremendous aspect, and frantic demeanour; and, descending to the level of common life, conversed with man as his equal" (Beattie 97). In other words, prose fiction separated into two broad genres – the romance and the novel – as the Enlightenment concern for the particular and the specific reconfigured the classical and neo-classical respect for the general and universal. Beattie hammers home the importance of probability throughout his essay. In a discussion of ancient prose fables and parables, Beattie insists that the forgotten progenitors of these folk stories adhered, as much as possible, to the law of probability (Beattie 4–5). This kind of probability is perhaps better described as internal coherence: Beattie claims that a fable can depict a talking animal, but probability has its limits: "nature should not be violated; nor the properties of one animal or vegetable ascribed to a different one" (Beattie 4). Later, Beattie criticizes "eastern tales" because "little regard would be paid to truth; and none at all to probability, or even to possibility, in their fables" (Beattie 27) and medieval romances come under fire for the same faults: "nature, probability, and even possibility, were not much attended to, in those compositions" (Beattie 91). In his discussion of modern prose fiction, Beattie praises Defoe's *Robinson Crusoe* for its adherence to the appearance of reality[12], while chastising Smollett for consistently painting "humorous pictures . . . exaggerated beyond all bounds of probability" (Beattie 108). Fielding receives high praise for his ability to plot a narrative in which "circumstances are all so natural, and rise so easily from one another" (Beattie 111). For Beattie, probability is a crucial element in prose fiction;

---

[12] Beattie speculates, with good reason, that Defoe's narrative of Crusoe's adventures is at least partly based on the adventures of Scottish sailor Alexander Selkirk.

without it, the reader of modern romances "breeds a dislike to history, and all the substantial parts of knowledge; withdraws attention from nature, and truth; and fills the mind with extravagant thoughts" (Beattie 112). *Bienseance* and *vraisemblance* are not just matters of current taste for Beattie: he sees adherence to probability and realism as the primary links between fiction and useful application.

Beattie's description of the romance tradition's devolution into the novel is predicated on the idea of scale: Beattie focuses on the "gigantic size, tremendous aspect, and frantic demeanour" of the romance tradition in opposition to the common and everyday concerns of the novel. Other romantic-era novel critics follow his lead. Just two years after Beattie, in 1785, Clara Reeve delivered her well-known definition of the novel in very similar terms:

> The Romance is an heroic fable, which treats of fabulous persons and things. – The Novel is a picture of real life and manners, and of the times in which it is written. The Romance in lofty and elevated language, describes what never happened nor is likely to happen. – The Novel gives a familiar relation of such things, as pass every day before our eyes . . . and the perfection of it, is to represent every scene, in so easy and natural a manner, and to make them appear so probable, as to deceive us into a persuasion . . . that all is real, until we are affected by the joys or distresses, of the persons in the story, as if they were our own. (Reeve, Vol. 1 111)

Reeve's definition clearly covers the same ground as William Congreve's novel definition a century earlier. But Reeve's novel definition has proved to be paradigmatic in its insistence on a separation from the romance, invocation of realism, and conceptualization of vicarious reader response to novel texts: two centuries after Reeve penned her definition (elements of which were clearly borrowed from Samuel Johnson and James Beattie, among others), contemporary critics are still using a similar set of criteria. Brean Hammond and Shaun Reagan, for example, pared J. Paul Hunter's list of early novel characteristics down to eight central concepts. Among the eight characteristics cited by Hammond and Regan are "credibility and probability," "familiarity," and "empathy and vicariousness" (Hammond and Regan 25–26).

Other romantic-era critics do not necessarily include all three characteristics championed by Reeve: John Moore, for example, only explicitly mentions the idea of familiarity, claiming that "modern romances are or ought to be a representation of life and manners in the country where the scene is placed" (Moore xcii). In other places, though, Moore disparages the fantastical excesses of the romance tradition and clearly sees the novel – which he terms the "modern romance" – as largely free from such aesthetic blemishes.

Barbauld tells her readers that "a good novel is an epic in prose, with more of character and less (indeed in modern novels nothing) of the supernatural machinery" (Barbauld 3). Barbauld's rejection of supernatural elements, though, is a tacit endorsement of the novel's engagement with the commonplace and everyday, and as the essay draws to a close, she references the novel's power of the vicarious in the genre's ability "to win the attention from pain or vexatious occurrences, to take man from himself . . . and . . . make him forget the subject of his own complaints" (Barbauld 44–45).

Scott's theory of the novel exists largely within the framework laid out by his predecessors, and indeed, he seems at times resistant to the very idea of theorizing the genre. In his collection of biographical sketches of novelists that served as prefatory material to the *Ballantyne's Novelist's Library*, Scott attempts to downplay any expectations for his critical work: "It may be necessary to observe, that the Lives do not lay claim to the merit of much research, being taken from the most accessible materials; and that the Critical Opinions are such as have occurred without much or profound study" (Scott, advertisement to *Biographical Notices*). Nevertheless, Scott does theorize about the novel. At the outset of his "Essay on Romance," Scott develops a familiar definition of the genre: "we would rather define [the novel] as 'a fictitious narrative, differing from the romance, because the events are accommodated to the ordinary train of human events, and the modern state of society'" (Scott, "Essay on Romance" 65). But Scott's understanding of the novel is deceptively simple. He argues that some fiction "partake[s] of the nature of both" (Scott, "Essay on Romance" 65) the romance and novel traditions, thus creating a definition that makes room for gothic fiction and his own historical romances. Scott, like the other critics under examination here, sees the development of a realistic prose fiction concerned with the common and ordinary events of everyday life as the natural result of the progress of western civilization, and in particular, British society: "the public taste growing more fastidious as the language became more copious, and the system of manners more complicated, graces of style and variety of sentiment were demanded instead of a naked and unadorned tale of wonders" (Scott, "Essay on Romance" 89). Scott is most concerned with the idea of realism in his theory of the novel. At the close of his "Essay on Romance," he pauses briefly to acknowledge that the ideal of realism – what in *belles lettres* rhetoric might be called *vraisemblance* – reached an apex with Defoe's *Robinson Crusoe*, in which "De Foe rendered fiction more impressive than truth itself" (Scott, "Essay on Romance" 108). For Scott, realism is the key to the novel's separation from romance.

John Colin Dunlop's understanding of the relationship of realism to the novel presented in *The History of Fiction* is, perhaps, the most complex, forward-looking, and – frustratingly – the least explicit. He begins by stating his intention to delineate "the origin and progress of fiction" and to "consider the different fictions in prose, which have been given to the world under the name of romance or novel" (Dunlop 9). Dunlop's declaration is not intended to conflate the two genres; rather, he is simply acknowledging that any history of fiction must include both genres. The distinction between the two, though, remains murky throughout Dunlop's text and the difference between them is referenced only obliquely. But Dunlop clearly sees a difference between fiction of the previous century (beginning, roughly, with Manley, Behn, and Haywood) and the fiction of preceding eras. In fact, Dunlop's entire theory of fiction is predicated on the differences between prose fiction of different times and places. Dunlop argues that because fiction is a universal literary mode, we should expect prose fiction to reflect the taste, values, interests, and morality of the specific historical and cultural context in which it is written (Dunlop 7–11). But Dunlop clearly sees what he terms the "modern novel" of the eighteenth century as an improvement over earlier examples of prose fiction. In his discussion of Greek romance, Dunlop draws a dividing line between fantastical romances and the realism of modern novels:

> One quality . . . [is] characteristic not only of Greek romance, but of the first attempt at prose fiction in any country: The interest of each work consists almost wholly in a succession of strange, and often improbable adventures . . . For the creation of these marvels sufficient scope was afforded [to the authors of ancient romances], because . . . the limits of probability were not precisely ascertained. (Dunlop 46)

Presumably, Dunlop believes that the limits of probability are much more firmly established at the beginning of the nineteenth century, thanks to centuries of progress which – in his view – have culminated in the British Empire.

After invoking probability as a defining characteristic of non-romance prose fiction, Dunlop goes on to attribute the lack of realism in ancient and medieval romances to the extremely limited social opportunities for women: "The seclusion, also, of females in these early times gave a certain uniformity to existence, and prevented the novelist from painting those minute and almost imperceptible traits of feeling and character, all those developments, which render a well-written modern novel so agreeable and interesting" (Dunlop 46). In other words, Dunlop argues that fiction which featured psychological detail and precise accounts of everyday life was not possible until women achieved a greater degree of social independence and intellectual opportunity. Thus he begins his discussion of British fiction with Manley, Behn, and Haywood, women whose writing reflected a "demand for something of a lighter and less exalted description [than prior prose fiction], and, accordingly, to this period may be ascribed the origin of that species of composition which, fostered by the improving taste of succeeding times, has been gradually matured into the English novel" (Dunlop 409). The British novel as we know it, according to Dunlop, was not a possibility before women were allowed some measure of access to socially acceptable venues of public discourse.

Dunlop was serious about his appreciation of women writers' contributions to the development of British prose fiction in the eighteenth century. He names Manley, Behn, and Haywood as the first three authors who produced recognizably contemporary British novels and goes on to praise the fiction of Fanny Burney, Barbauld's criticism, Frances Sheridan's *Sidney Bidulph*, Clara Reeve's *The Old English Baron*, and all of Ann Radcliffe's novels. His praise for Radcliffe in particular recalls his comments about the deficiencies of ancient romances: "Mrs. Radcliffe was capable of painting, not merely the general features of the personages in a romance, but the finer traits of character in a novel of real life" (Dunlop 417).

But the presence of women – especially as consumers of novels – brings attention to the third major point of congruence among these early theories of the novel: the novel's utility in inculcating virtue, morality, and social values in its readers. Constructing an acceptable literary pedigree and articulating the novel's focus on realistic portrayals of everyday life could only go so far in establishing the genre as respectable and worthy of serious attention. In fact, the realism of novels was a liability to many critics. Samuel Johnson, for example, worried that novels were more dangerous to the morals and values of naïve and inexperienced readers – especially young women – because, unlike the unbelievable fantastical excesses of romances, novels presented life as it actually was and thus created the possibility of glorifying socially unacceptable behaviors and lifestyles while attempting to criticize them (Johnson 177 – 179). Terry Eagleton sums up this conundrum in *The English Novel*:

> There is . . . [a] problem with the novel's very closeness to social existence. If the novel is a 'slice of life', how can it teach us more general truths? This is a particular problem for devoutly Protestant eighteenth-century authors like Samuel Richardson, for whom the artifice of fiction is only really justified if it conveys a moral truth . . . The dilemma is that the more graphic you make your realism, the more this drives the moral truth home; but the more it simultaneously undermines it, since the reader becomes more attentive to the realist detail than to the universal truth it is meant to exemplify. (Eagleton 12)

Eagleton further observes that writers like Richardson were well aware of this problem:

> Writing of his novel *Clarissa*, Richardson comments that he wants nothing in its Preface which would *prove* that the work was fiction, but that he does not want it to be *thought* genuine either... The reader must not be told that the book is fiction, since this might undermine its power. But if readers genuinely take it to be real, this in turn might diminish its exemplary force (Eagleton 13).

This quandary, though, was perhaps unavoidable. John J. Richetti argues that the novel's increased emphasis on realism made the question of morality and virtue unavoidable: "For the novel, the ordinary and the specifically and concretely experiential (along with the everyday language specific to that realm) come in this new world of narrative to define the absolute boundaries or limits of reality and by extension of moral significance" (Richetti 4). The emphasis on realism, then, forces an examination of morality. In the romance tradition, full of dragons and monsters and magic, questions about virtue and vice do not impinge on the narrative with the same force as in the realistic and everyday novel.

This problem, as Eagleton has observed, was understood by the novelists of the long eighteenth century. In the dedication to *Oroonoko*, Aphra Behn rests her apology for the text's subject matter on the idea that "Virtue is a noble Lesson to be learn'd, and 'tis by Comparison we can Judge and Chuse" (Behn 6). Behn is arguing that in *Oroonoko*, virtue is demonstrated in contrast to vice and that it is the reader's responsibility to recognize and choose between the two. Eagleton rightly points to Richardson's concern that his work should walk a fine line, on one side of which lies a dearth of realism and on the other the dangers of realism run amok. The preface to *Pamela* exhibits this concern: Richardson hopes to "*divert* and *entertain*" while managing to "*instruct* and *improve* the minds of the YOUTH of *both sexes*;" furthermore, Richardson intends to "paint VICE in its proper colours, to make it deservedly odious; and to set VIRTUE in its own amiable light, to make it look lovely" (Richardson 31). Richardson continues, explaining that reading *Pamela* will be profitable because the text will cast religion and morality in a "delightful and profitable" light, leading to a further discussion of justice, financial responsibility, and marriage, all without ever "raising a *single idea* throughout the whole, that shall shock the exactest purity, even in the warmest of those instances where Purity would be most apprehensive" (31). Richardson intends that there should be no mistake about his novel: it is a deliberately moral and virtuous text intended to impart such lessons to its readers.

Other well-known examples are found in the work of Daniel Defoe and Henry Fielding. Defoe's line of defense is direct and straightforward. In *Moll*

Flanders, Defoe begins by apologizing at some length for the story presented in its pages:

> The Pen employ'd in finishing her Story, and making it what you now see it to be, has had no little difficulty to put it into a Dress fit to be seen, and to make it speak Language fit to be read: When a Woman debauch'd from her Youth . . . comes to give an Account of all her vicious Practices, and even to descend to the particular Occasions and Circumstances by which she first became wicked, and of all the progression of Crime which she run through . . . an Author must be hard put to it to wrap it up so clean, as not to give room, especially for vicious Readers to turn it to his Disadvantage . . . To give the History of a wicked Life repented of, necessarily requires that the wicked Part should be made as wicked as the real History of it will bear, to illustrate and give a Beauty to the Penitent part, which is certainly the best and brightest. (Defoe 37–38)

Defoe understands the inverse relationship between realism and moral effect described by Eagleton, at one point offering his hope that readers of *Moll Flanders* "will be much more pleas'd with the Moral than the Fable, with the Application than with the Relation, and with the End of the Writer that with the Life of the Person written of" (Defoe 38–39).

Toward the novel's conclusion as Moll begins to live a staid, penitent, and prosperous life, Moll herself explains that she is disgusted by her history of sins, misdeeds, and crimes; furthermore, the reader should be as well:

> I reflect that many of those who may be pleas'd and diverted with the Relation of the wild and wicked part of my Story, may not relish this, which is really the best part of my Life, the most Advantageous to myself, and the most instructive to others . . . It would be a severe Satyr on such, to say they do not relish the Repentance as much as they do the Crime. (Defoe 369)

Moll makes such statements with some frequency as she realizes that the recitation of her life may not have the intended effect: her escapades, which eventually all turn to her advantage, might have the unintended and undesirable effect of encouraging vice while obscuring her repentance and turn toward a moral and virtuous life.

Henry Fielding also demonstrates a keen awareness of this problem, but his response is somewhat more complex than Defoe's. In the preface to *Joseph Andrews*, Fielding includes a preemptive strike against the potential critics whom he imagines will be critical of the novel's presentation of vice:

> But perhaps it may be objected to me, that I have . . . introduced vices, and of a very black kind into this work. To which I shall answer . . . that

> it is very difficult to pursue a series of human actions and keep clear from them . . . [T]hey are never the principal figure at that time on the scene; and lastly, they never produce the intended evil. (Fielding, *Joseph Andrews* 47)

Fielding understands what Richetti makes clear: realistic fiction forces questions about morality and virtue to the fore. The question for Fielding is how to develop fiction that is true to the lived experience of ordinary people without glorifying vice in the process.

Fielding addresses the issue of realism's troubled relationship with teaching virtue and glorifying vice more explicitly in the preface to *Jonathan Wild*. While admitting that everyone is familiar with the lurid historical details of the famous outlaw's exploits, Fielding hopes to present a "narrative . . . rather of such actions which he might have performed, or would, or should have performed" (Fielding, *Jonathan Wild* 29). But the major problem with the text has nothing to do with historical veracity. Fielding knows that writing about the life of a notorious criminal invites criticism and censure, and he answers potential critics by making it clear that glorification of vice is hardly his intention. His defense of *Jonathan Wild*, in fact, addresses Eagleton's question concerning how specific and particular events can cast light on general and universal principles:

> I do by no means intend in the character of my hero to represent nature in general . . . For my part, I understand those writers who describe human nature in this depraved character, as speaking only of such persons as Wild and his gang; and I think it may be justly inferred, that they do not find in their own bosoms any deviation from the general rule. Indeed it would be an insufferable vanity in them to conceive themselves as the exception to it. (Fielding, Preface to *Jonathan Wild* 29–30)

Fielding believes that novels can only effectively communicate moral, universal truths when the characters populating novels are intended – within their specificities and particularities – to exist as general examples masquerading as particular individuals.

Just as concerns about virtue and morality were manifested in eighteenth-century novels, the theories of the novel in the romantic era also discussed the importance of virtue in prose fiction. Throughout these novel theories, morality and didactic purpose are cited as criteria for judging texts: morality was as important a criterion as probability and realism. For Beattie, this concept is foundational, since he argues that fiction in all forms has been used, since the beginning of recorded history, to teach lessons and convey cultural values[13] (Beattie 2). Beattie's assessment of individual novels is often predicated entirely on their moral and didactic function: a novel might be interesting, entertaining, probable, and true-to-life, but if the moral content is problematic, the novel is not worth reading. In his criticism of Richardson, Beattie objects to Richardson's portrayal of immoral characters: "like most other novel writers, he represents some of his wicked characters as more agreeable than was necessary to his plan, which may make the example dangerous" (Beattie 104). Eagleton's description of the inverse relationship of realism to the effective portrayal of virtue and vice is at the heart of Beattie's concerns:

> [W]hen a character . . . whom the reader ought to abominate for his crimes, is adorned with youth, beauty, eloquence, wit, and every other intellectual and bodily accomplishment, it is to be tempted to imitate, even while they disapprove him . . . The reader knows that the story is a fiction: but he know too, that such talents and qualities, if they were to appear in real life, would be irresistibly engaging . . . Is there not, then, reason to apprehend, that some readers will be more inclined to admire the gay profligate than to fear his punishment? (Beattie 105)

Here, Beattie makes a tacit, though crucial, distinction between the novel and other genres: the realism of the novel makes it more dangerous to the morals of its readers than any other literary form. Specifically, Beattie complains that in Richardson's *Clarissa*, Lovelace's crimes and faults are not epic in scale and so they are not punished sufficiently. Beattie laments that the story would have been "more useful in a moral view, and perhaps more interesting" if Lovelace had either come to complete ruin or been brought, through "probable means" to "an exemplary repentance" (Beattie 106).

Morality and probability – inextricably linked, as Eagleton and Richetti confirm – are the key criteria for Beattie. Regarding Smollett, Beattie criticizes the lack of probability and censures even more forcefully the morality of *Roderick Random, Peregrine Pickle*, and the rest, calling them "inexcusably licentious" and populated by "[p]rofligates, bullies, and misanthropes" (Beattie 108). Fielding does not escape on this count: *Joseph Andrews* suffers from "passages [which] offend by their indelicacy" (Beattie 110) and *Tom Jones* would have been much improved if Fielding had not described some of Tom's exploits with such detail and precision (Beattie 110). None of this, though, prevents Beattie from praising the artistry of Fielding's novels.

---

[13] The use of fiction to teach a lesson or illustrate a concept was presented as part of a formal theory of argument at least as far back as Aristotle, who includes fictitious narratives as a mode of artistic persuasion in Book Two of his *Rhetoric*.

Tom Jones and *Amelia* are praised as "the most perfect, perhaps, of their kind in the world" (Beattie 111). Beattie's assessment of Fielding is thus conflicted because while Fielding's novels are perfect examples of the genre, they are flawed regarding their usefulness for instruction, and in the end, Beattie's assessment of the genre is overwhelmingly pessimistic. After one hundred twelve pages of writing about fables, romances, and modern romances, Beattie warns his readers, "Let not the usefulness of romance writing be estimated by the length of my discourse upon it" (Beattie 112). The final judgment on the genre is clear and direct: "Romances are a dangerous recreation. A few, no doubt, of the best may be friendly to good taste and good morals; but far the greater part are unskillfully written, and tend to corrupt the heart, and stimulate the passions" (Beattie 112).

Only two years after Beattie, Reeve presents a forceful defense of novels that rests on three belletristic criteria: genius, taste, and morality. Like Beattie, Reeve is concerned that young, inexperienced, and uninformed readers might not make good decisions about their reading material. Unlike Beattie, Reeve is thoroughly optimistic about the potential for novels to convey morality and virtue. While Beattie bluntly warns that "Romances are a dangerous recreation" (Beattie 112), Reeve offers unquestionable – though carefully qualified – praise for the genre: "[U]nder proper restrictions and regulations they will afford much useful instruction, as well as rational and elegant amusement. In this view therefore they are equally entitled to our attention and respect, as any other works of Genius and literature" (Reeve xvi). In the first evening's dialogue, Reeve admits that novels, read without any regard for good taste or correct judgment "are at best unprofitable, frequently productive of absurdities in manners and sentiments, sometimes hurtful to good morals" (Reeve, vol. I 7).

But Reeve's view of the genre is mostly positive. She argues that there is much to be gained from selecting and reading the best novels: "from this Genus there may be selected books that are truly respectable, works of genius, taste, and utility, capable of improving the morals and manners of mankind" (Reeve, vol. I 7). Unlike Beattie, Reeve is not simply setting forth a history of the genre with critical observations on some of the more familiar texts. Reeve is much more ambitious: she intends to develop a full-fledged theory of the genre. In the dialogue of Evening I, Reeve observes that prose fiction has yet to be properly theorized; the genre "wants to be methodized, to be separated, classed, and regulated" (Reeve, vol. I 8). Reeve's purpose is clearly to defend the genre through "remark[ing] upon the most eminent works of the kind, and [paying] tribute . . . to works of Genius and morality" (Reeve, vol. I 9). Reeve defends the novel based on its artistic merits and moral utility, though the latter criterion is clearly the more important of the two.

Throughout her defense of ancient, medieval, and renaissance romance, Reeve consistently defends the best examples of the genre because "these stories . . . have a moral tendency [and] they go frequently much higher, and when composed by people of cultivated genius and virtuous principles, they speak to all the noblest feelings of the human heart" (Reeve, vol. I 97). When she turns her attention to the more recent development of the novel, Reeve's criticism often focuses entirely on the moral content of a text. Behn is praised for "strong marks of Genius" but is condemned for including material that might be harmful to "virtuous minds, and especially to youth" (Reeve, vol. I 117). Manley lacks Behn's genius and the moral content of her fiction is even more questionable, to the point that Reeve refuses to mention her texts by name (Reeve, vol. I 119). Haywood is forgiven for her improprieties because "she repented of her faults;" nevertheless, she wrote amatory fiction in her youth which was immortalized in Pope's *Dunciad* and that may be her unfortunate legacy (Reeve, vol. I 120–121). Reeve's assessment of Defoe's *Robinson Crusoe* and Berkeley's *Guadentio di Lucca* praises the originality of both texts. Much better than originality, though, is the moral content of the two novels:

> [W]hat gives a still higher value to these two books . . . [is that] they are evidently written to promote the cause of religion and virtue, and may safely be put into the hands of youth. Such books cannot be too strongly recommended, as under the disguise of fiction, warm the heart with the love of virtue, and by than means, excited the reader to the practice of it. (Reeve, vol. I 125 – 126)

Moral content again comes to the fore when Reeve turns to Richardson and Fielding. Richardson is without equal in Reeve's assessment because of the moral utility of *Pamela*. Fielding is artistically very good, but Reeve "consider[s] wit only as a secondary merit," and thus, Fielding's works are "as much inferior to Richardson's in moral and exemplary characters, as they are superior in wit and learning" (Reeve, vol. I 139). Reeve, like Beattie, also makes note of the danger of presenting vice in a too casual or pleasant manner. *Tom Jones* is particularly at fault in this regard. Yet Fielding's indiscretions are mitigated because virtue always receives due respect in his novels; furthermore, Fielding "painted human nature *as it is*, rather than as *it ought to be*" (Reeve, vol. I 141).

In Volume II of *The Progress of Romance*, Reeve continues to pass judgment on novels of the preceding hundred years. Smollett is criticized for exceeding the limits of probability, but his work is lauded for their "moral tendency," though they contain "some scenes that are not proper for all readers" (Reeve, vol. II 10). Frances Sheridan's *Sidney Bidulph* receives cautious praise: the novel's intentions are good, but the text has a "gloomy tendency" that might distort its presentation of virtue (Reeve, vol. II 25). Reeve continues to catalogue, analyze, and offer recommendations for the balance of the text. In all, Reeve mentions more than fifty different novelists and more than sixty individual novels. While she mentions probability, genius, wit, and other factors that might determine the worthiness of a title, of paramount importance is the text's moral content. Midway through Volume II, Reeve forcefully establishes morality as the prime criterion for judging novels: "I refused to admit works of prophaneness [sic] and immorality into my Catalogue of eminent Novels, though admired for their wit, or for the name of the Authors; I should be concerned to have occasion to repeat any more what I have said on this subject" (Reeve, vol. II 36).

But while morality is of paramount importance to Reeve, she is equally clear that morality is not enough to recommend a novel. In the dialogue from Evening X, Reeve, through Euphrasia, responds to a question about the merits of Margaret Minifie's novels: "They are in the class of mediocrity . . . I must therefore pass over these, and hundreds beside that are very innocent and moral books" (Reeve, vol. II 46). The lack of morality may automatically disqualify a title from Reeve's approval, but the lack of artistic merit also damns a text to faint praise and relegation to a class of innocent, but mediocre novels.

As Reeve draws *The Progress of Romance* to a close, she repeats her critical refrain – genius, taste, and morality – half a dozen times. But, more than genius or taste, Reeve's theory of the novel is a theory of fiction and moral purpose. Almost every text Reeve mentions is selected or rejected for its morality, or lack thereof. She drives this point home and sums up her theory of the novel in a quotation from a now long-forgotten late eighteenth-century novel, *The Trial, or the History of Charles Horton, esq*[14]:

> If you wish in a Novel to inculcate some moral truth . . . there should always be a reference to the manners of the time in which it is written; there should be the greatest probability, carried thro the whole allegory,

---

[14] The entire quote is three pages long and goes into some detail about why novels are particularly effective in teaching morality and virtue. The anonymous author concludes, like Blair and Barbauld, that novels have political power: "[W]ere I a despotic prince, I would sooner hang an author that wrote a work that had a direct or indirect tendency to corrupt the morals of the youthful, and consequently the most part of my subjects, than I would whip a man, who, impelled by absolute necessity, should commit a robbery on the high road" (*The Trial* 34–35).

that your reason may not be shocked, while your imagination is pleased. If novels were properly regulated with this design always in view, they might become really useful to society. (*The Trial* qtd. in Reeve, vol. II 92).

Communicating moral truth in fiction requires a novelist to develop and deploy probability and realism: without these two elements, the moral purpose of a novel is lost. Without morality, though, all the artistry of verisimilitude is wasted effort.

John Moore's assessment of instructive value of novels echoes Beattie's view: fiction is the best way to communicate morals and values to readers who lack the intellectual ability or self-discipline to receive lessons from works of "pure science and instruction" (Moore xciv). Like Beattie, Moore believes fiction has instructional utility primarily for the obdurate and uneducated masses most in need of instruction: "Persons of dissipated minds, incapable of attention, who stand most in need of instruction, are the least willing to receive it; they throw such books down the moment they perceive their drift" (Moore xciv). But entertaining fiction, with a "moral intention" is capable of slipping past the defenses of such a reader and teaching morality and virtue whether the reader likes it or not (Moore xciv). Regarding particular novels, Moore focuses on Richardson, Fielding, and Smollett. Like Beattie and Reeve before him, Moore worries that Richardson's moral intentions may have been superseded by his brilliant description of the despicable Lovelace in *Clarissa* (Moore lxxxix). Fielding's *Tom Jones* is regarded as worthy of merit, as is Smollett, though this is to be expected, since Moore is writing a preface to his edition of Smollett's works.

Barbauld's conception of the novel also places didactive function at the forefront. Barbauld begins her essay by describing the near-universal pleasures novel reading affords: genius, propriety, and stylistic excellence are all cited as crucial to a novel's successful reception. But Barbauld concludes her early description of the novel's merits by turning her attention to the possibilities for moral instruction offered by prose fiction: "[T]he power exercised over the reader's heart by filling it with the successive emotions of love, pity, joy, anguish, transport, or indignation, together with the grave impressive moral resulting from the whole, imply talents of the highest order, and ought to be appreciated accordingly" (Barbauld 2–3). Her assessments of individual novels often revolve around questions of virtue and morality. *Gil Blas* is found to be entertaining, though morally dubious (Barbauld 17); Aphra Behn's fiction is dismissed as "licentious" and "fallen" (Barbauld 35); *The Adventures of a Guinea* is praised for the accurate portrayal of everyday life, though "many of the scenes are too coarse not to offend a delicate mind" (Barbauld 38). Sterne comes under severe censure: although the artistry of his fiction is undeniable, "the indelicacies of these volumes are very reprehensible, and indeed in a clergyman scandalous" (Barbauld 39). Barbauld judges novels by their attention to probability and realism, but she clearly finds the lack of moral purpose inexcusable.

Unlike Reeve, though, Barbauld sees moral improvement of secondary importance to the true purpose of novels: entertainment and diversion. To be sure, morality is of great importance. But to Barbauld, it is enough if a novel simply does no harm and still manages to entertain. Entertainment is the highest value for a novel to attain: "The unpardonable sin of a novel is dullness: however grave or wise it may be, if its author possesses no powers of amusing, he has no business to write novels" (Barbauld 45). Amusement is not the only quality that novels offer, though: "It is impossible to deny that the most glowing and impressive sentiments of virtue are to be found in many of these compositions, and have been deeply imbibed by their youthful readers" (Barbauld 46) and furthermore, "[w]hen works of fancy are thus made subservient to the improvement of the rising generation, they certainly stand on a higher ground than mere entertainment, and we revere what we admire" (Barbauld 48). In the end, though, the usefulness of novel reading depends on the taste and judgment of the reader. The novel reader must be able to make reasonably well-informed decisions about his or her choice of reading material for novels to provide entertainment and morality without compromising the reader's values and virtues.

But Barbauld believes novels to be capable of much more than teaching lessons about virtue. Barbauld clearly sees novels as capable of affecting the beliefs and judgments at a national level: when she invokes Andrew Fletcher at the end of her essay, Barbauld goes beyond Blair's passive acknowledgement that novels might be influential. Novels, Barbauld declares, can change the course of a nation's cultural and social destiny. When she closes her essay by stating "Let me make the novels of a country, and let who will make the systems" (Barbauld 59), Barbauld is claiming a far-reaching didactive function for the novel: the broad popularity of novels – combined with their power to entertain, elevate the emotions, vicariously move the reader, and teach virtue and morality – makes the prose fiction of Barbauld's era a political force. Barbauld clearly understands that the power to theorize and canonize the novel is also the power to shape the culture of the nation for generations to come.

Unlike Beattie, Reeve, Moore, and Barbauld, J.C. Dunlop makes few explicit references to morality in his general theory of the novel. Early in Dunlop's *The History of Fiction*, he announces that fiction is perhaps most useful in its ability to provide a "successive delineation of . . . prevalent modes of thinking, a picture of their feelings and tastes and habits;" in addition, Dunlop observes that even without the utility of fiction, readers of fiction are "indebted to it for pleasure and enjoyment" (Dunlop 8). But Dunlop makes no general pronouncements about the place or importance of moral content or didactive function in relation to the novel. However, when he discusses specific texts, morality is clearly a concern. Behn is described as failing to avoid the "moral contagion which infected the literature of that age" (Dunlop 409). Heywood falls under the same approbation, though *Betsy Thoughtless* mitigates the issue. Richardson's *Clarissa* is praised for exhibiting "the great moral . . . that in every situation virtue is triumphant" (Dunlop 411); furthermore, "the object of Richardson, in all his novels, is to show the superiority of virtue" (Dunlop 411). William Godwin's *Caleb Williams* is lauded for Falkland's "visionary principles of honour" (Dunlop 412). Dunlop's only criticism of Fielding is that, in *Tom Jones*, he regrettably allows Tom to have illegitimate parentage, a moral defect that Dunlop believes Fielding could – and should – have done without (Dunlop 413). Smollett is also praised for the virtuous nature of his novels, especially *Humphrey Clinker* which "confirm[s] strongly the great moral truth, that happiness and all our feelings are the result, less of external circumstances, than the constitution of the mind" (Dunlop 413). Gothic fiction is noted to have a "general tendency" toward virtue and finally, *Robinson Crusoe* is placed at the forefront of great fiction because "of all the works of fiction that have ever been composed, *Robinson Crusoe* is perhaps the most interesting and instructive" (Dunlop 418–419). The cumulative effect of Dunlop's criticism of individual titles is clear, though: morality matters in determining the value of a novel.

Scott's take on morality is, like Dunlop's, tied primarily to individual titles and not to a larger theory of the novel. Predictably, Scott praises Richardson, Fielding, Smollett, Goldsmith, Reeve, Radcliffe, and many more for the generally moral tone of their fiction. But Scott sees morality as potentially detrimental to the aesthetic of the fiction: focusing on morality instead of artistry is a perilous fault for a novelist. In his discussion of Samuel Richardson, Scott makes note of Richardson's moral intentions, but questions such an instinct. Regarding *Clarissa,* Scott observes that "the direct and obvious moral to be deduced from a fictitious narrative, is of much less consequence to the public, than the mode in which the story is treated in the course of its details" (Scott, *Notices* 29). Scott even goes so far as to question the effectiveness of novels in teaching morality and virtue. Regarding Fielding's work, Scott defends the more questionable passages by arguing that the presentation of vice had rarely, if ever, created one more ne'er do well who would not have become one *without* reading Fielding (Scott, *Notices* 78). But Scott wavers on this point: in passing judgment on Smollett's *Ferdinand, Count Fathom,* he criticizes Smollett for creating, in the Count, "a disgusting pollution of the imagination" (Scott, *Notices* 97). Furthermore, Scott warns the reader that writing like

Smollett's might encourage naïve and inexperienced readers to emulate, rather than despise, such a character (Scott, *Notices* 97). But Scott does not put morality on the same level as aesthetics in his assessment of prose fiction. Instead, Scott, like Barbauld before him, sees morality as desirable in fiction, yet believes that novels should primarily entertain while endeavoring to do no harm.

Assessing Romantic-Era Theories of the Novel

Generalizing the theories of the novel presented by these critics is relatively simple work: the novel is prose fiction related to (but separate from) the romance tradition, marked by an attention to the commonplace and everyday as its subject matter and a rejection of the fantastical and marvelous, and useful in its ability to communicate virtue, morality, and social values, though potentially dangerous in its tendency to affect the emotions and sentiments of its readers while often inadvertently presenting vice as more attractive than virtue. The question, then, is how *belles lettres* fits into the description of these theories of the novel. To put it simply: *belles lettres* is the structuring principle of romantic-era theories of the novel.

The first place to look for the presence of *belles lettres* in the novel theory of the romantic era is in the language used by the critics who theorized about the novel. Over and over, the same terms are used: propriety (a concept which includes the concepts of probability, possibility, and verisimilitude), genius, taste, morality, virtue, and vice are all particular and specific terms within belletristic rhetorical theory. Barbara Warnick's *The Sixth Canon* makes this exceptionally clear. *Belles lettres*, as established in eighteenth-century British rhetorical theory, advanced an aesthetic concerned with propriety, sublimity, and taste (Warnick 5). Golden and Corbett consider a similar set of concepts – taste, style, criticism, and sublimity – in their introduction to *The Rhetoric of Blair, Campbell, and Whately* (Golden and Corbett 8).

These concepts were present in the earliest development of *belles lettres* in the Scottish universities. The earliest formal lectures on *belles lettres* in Britain were delivered by Adam Smith at the University of Edinburgh, beginning in 1748. Smith's lectures are aggressive about propriety in discourse. In Lecture 11, Smith defines propriety in discourse as "Expressing in the most concise, proper and precise manner the thought of the author, and that in the manner which best conveys the sentiment, passion or affection with which it affects . . . [the author] and which he designs to communicate to his reader" (Smith 55). Smith's approach to propriety in discourse becomes, in Blair's lectures, a catch-all critical concept for judging any form of discourse, novels included.

To Blair, propriety is of central importance in the development of taste: without an understanding of propriety, proper taste cannot form. For example, Blair argues that good taste allows us to draw pleasure from reading *The Æneid*: "[A] great part of our pleasure arises from the plan or story being well conducted, and all the parts joined together with probability and due connexion; from characters being taken from nature, the sentiments suited to the characters, and the style to the sentiments" (Blair 13). Propriety and taste concern the internal unity of a text and the expectations which a reader might have concerning the text.

Blair's example demonstrates *belles lettres* rhetoric's central preoccupation with propriety and probability in the judgment of any literary text. But when *belles lettres* is applied to the novel, the critical paradigm for assessing novels for the next century crystallizes:

> Imitations of life and character have been made their [the recent novels] principal object. Relations have been professed to be given of the behavior of persons in particular interesting situations, such as may actually occur in life; by means of which, what is laudable or defective in character and in conduct, may be pointed out, and placed in an useful light. (Blair 423)

Blair is arguing that novels are an instance of epideictic rhetoric, an ancient rhetorical concept which concerns discourse intended to "praise or blame . . . what was honorable or dishonorable" (Kennedy 7). Praising virtue and blaming vice – in discourse as well as in human behavior – is central to the *belles lettres* theory of criticism Blair develops in his *Lectures*. Virtue and vice are also crucial components in the romantic-era theories of the novel examined in this chapter.

The novel theories offered by Beattie, Reeve, Moore, Barbauld, and Dunlop are primarily concerned with two concepts: ethics and aesthetics. By ethics, I mean that these critics make the moral content of a text a central component in their judgment of the text. Aesthetics means that these critics also make judgments about texts based on a specific set of aesthetic expectations – typically including probability and everyday subject matter – that are accepted as the primary descriptive and distinguishing characteristics of the novel genre. The relationship between ethics and aesthetics is the basis for romantic-era theories of the novel: novels might be full of well-plotted events, vivid and familiar characters, and clear, well-crafted prose, but the suitability of a novel depends also on its moral fitness. Propriety – the master concept in *belles lettres* – extends beyond style and subject matter: propriety exists in the proper balance between aesthetic achievement and moral force; thus, novels are praised and dismissed based on both their aesthetic and ethical merits. Barbauld and Scott, at one end of the spectrum, argue that novels must entertain their readers and do them no harm; Beattie and Reeve, at the other end, argue the entertainment value of novels is justified primarily because of their utility in teaching morality and values. The relationship of ethics and aesthetics is a foundational concept in *belles lettres*: the moral and the beautiful are simply two sides of the same coin.

As Linda Ferreira-Buckley and S. Michael Halloran argue, "the beauty of *belles lettres* was understood by Blair and his contemporaries . . . to have moral significance" (Ferreira-Buckley and Halloran XXXVIII). Furthermore:

> The connection derived from theories that postulated a common source for moral and aesthetic judgments, an inner sense of rightness that estimated both conduct and discourse according to principles of proportion and balance that in one domain constituted goodness, in another beauty. By developing his students' ability to write beautifully and to appreciate the beauties of others' writings, Blair thus understood himself to be helping them grow as moral beings. (Ferreira-Buckley and Halloran XXXVIII)

The moral dimension of *belles lettres* and Blair's work in particular is indisputable. Thomas P. Miller asserts that Blair "helped popularize the values of sensibility, sociability, and the other moderate virtues that maintain the proprieties of civil society" and further, Blair and other belletrists "encouraged readers to look inward, reflect on their responses to experience, and learn self-restraint by refining their tastes" (Blair 249). Such an approach to criticism is clearly evident in the novel theories examined in this chapter.

Beattie, for example, concludes "On Fable and Romance" by cautioning that most prose fiction is harmful, both for aesthetic reasons and ethical reasons: romances are "unskillfully written, and tend to corrupt the heart" (Beattie 112). Reeve ambitiously states her desire to help novel readers choose correctly; if she succeeds in her attempt, she will "have performed the duties of a good citizen of the Republic of letters" (Reeve, vol. II 98). Barbauld, in typically straightforward fashion, defends the length of her essay by stating that "a discriminating taste is no where more called for than with regard to a species of books which everybody reads" (Barbauld 59), a statement, of course, which clearly echoes Blair's defense of novel criticism in his *Lectures*. The instinct to provide a basis for making correct judgments about novel reading choices is at its core a belletristic outgrowth of Blair's attempt to develop taste and judgment in a general theory of discourse. The possession of taste and judgment thus implies the ability to choose correctly. These choices manifest themselves in the formation of the novel canon during the romantic era.

Romantic-era Novel Canons

Earlier in this chapter, I acknowledged various contingencies which certainly played a part in the development of a canon of British novels during the romantic era. William St. Clair describes the economic and legal realities, and Claudia Johnson illuminates some of the cultural and social factors which influenced the emergence of the novel canon. Both scholars represent their critical viewpoint quite effectively, and there were any number of economic, legal, social, and cultural components which had an effect on the formation of the novel canon. But after a close examination of the novel histories and theories of the romantic era, the influence of *belles lettres* certainly deserves to be considered as well. The belletristic interest in genius and the formation of taste through contact with the best examples of various modes of discourse naturally leads to the formation of a canon: reading the best and most representative novels developed taste through the growth of moral sense and aesthetic appreciation.

With these ideas in mind, I have constructed a romantic-era novel canon drawn from the texts examined in this chapter. My method was simple and pragmatic: as I read each text, I made note of every author and title mentioned and, of course, whether the author and title were judged to be acceptable. Then I compared the author and title lists from all six texts. Any title I found mentioned in at least three of the six texts has been included as part of the Romantic-era novel canon. In the end, the canon established during the romantic era is remarkably uniform. As presented in the work of Beattie, Reeve, Moore, Barbauld, Dunlop, and Scott, the canon shows agreement on six non-English language and seventeen British novelists. The canon includes six women and seventeen men who produced texts as early as 1605 and as late as 1771. Most importantly, the Romantic-era novel canon developed in response to belletristic rhetorical principles that were at least as influential as any economic, social, cultural, or legal contingency.

A British Romantic Era Fiction Canon, 1780 – 1825[15]

Non-English Language Prose Fiction / Novel Canon
Cervantes, Miguel. *Don Quixote*. 1605 / 1615
Segrais, Jean. *Zayde*. 1670.
le Sage, Alain. *Gil Blas*. 1715 – 1735.
Riccoboni, Marie. Various. 1714 – 1792
Marivaux, Pierre de. *Paysan Parvenne*. 1735.
Rousseau, Jean-Jacques. *Eloisa*. 1761.

British Prose Fiction / Novel Canon
Barclay, John. *Argenis*. 1621.

---

[15] A full list of novels and prose fiction mentioned in the six studies reviewed in this chapter can be found in Appendix A.

"Let me make the novels"   99

Bunyan, John. *Pilgrim's Progress*. 1678.
Behn, Aphra. *Oroonoko*. 1688.
Manley, Delarivier. *Atalantis*. 1709.
Defoe, Daniel. *Robinson Crusoe*. 1719. et. al.
Swift, Jonathan. *Gulliver's Travels*. 1726.
Richardson, Samuel. *Pamela*. 1740. et. al.
Fielding, Henry. *Joseph Andrews*. 1741. et. al.
Smollett, Tobias. *Roderick Random*. 1748. et. al.
Haywood, Eliza. *Betsy Thoughtless*. 1751. et. al.
Lennox, Charlotte. *The Female Quixote*. 1752.
Johnson, Samuel. *Rasselas*. 1759.
Johnstone, Charles. Chrysal; or The Adventures of a Guinea. 1760
Sterne, Laurence. *Tristram Shandy* and *A Sentimental Journey*. 1759 / 1768.
Walpole, Horace. *The Castle of Otranto*. 1764.
Sheridan, Frances. *Sidney Bidulph*. 1767.
MacKenzie, Henry. *The Man of Feeling*. 1771.

What emerges from even a brief examination of such a canon is a simultaneous sense of inclusion and familiarity. *Robinson Crusoe* and *Pamela* are only to be expected, but Johnstone's *Adventures of a Guinea* is, perhaps, somewhat surprising. Behn and Manley emerge as the standard bearers for the early British novel, while sentimental and gothic fiction are well represented in the work of Sterne, Walpole, and MacKenzie[16]. The canon developed in the work of these six critics illustrates Trevor Ross' assertion that in the eighteenth century, "canon-making became less a form of symbolic gesturing . . . than a function of discourse," a shift which occurred "in accordance with a shift in emphasis in canon-making from production to consumption" (Ross 92).

Consumption is a concept rife with economic implications; however, rhetoric also shifted emphasis during the eighteenth century from production to consumption. Blair's *Lectures* are intended to aid the formation of proper judgment, and thus consumption of the right sort of texts. Scotland's marginalized

---

[16] Some texts that might be expected are absent for purely practical reasons. Reeve explicitly rejects the notion of evaluating the work of living authors (including herself), instead offering the hope that "the public will do them justice, and time will shew, whether they owed their success to intrisic [sic] merit, or to the caprice of fashion" (Reeve, Vol. II 100). Scott, writing in 1820, includes Reeve and Anne Radcliffe, neither of whom could have been included in Beattie's or Reeve's canons. Scott also undercuts the idea that his canon was intentionally more restrictive than Barbauld's. In the preface to *Notices Biographical and Critical*, Scott casually observes that the Ballantyne's Novelist's Library was intended to be a much larger collection; however, the death of John Ballantyne forced the discontinuation of the series (Scott, Advertisement to *Biographical and Critical Notices*).

position on the edges of cultural power meant that "Blair's provincial students and readers had to be formally taught the taste and style of the educated culture because they were not born and raised within it" (Miller 228). Blair's *belles lettres*, in other words, is intended to develop taste and judgment so that the reader might practice proper (and safe) consumption of any form of discourse, novels included. Canons functioned as an extension of this belletristic attempt to make educated culture accessible to the newly literate classes. Ross recognizes the culture-forming potential of canon-making, arguing that "the acquisition of cultural capital could be pursued through the ostensibly disinterested appreciation of aesthetic value" (Ross 92).

Familiarity with the canon, then, was of paramount importance to those individuals outside the cultural establishment who hoped to be granted access. Reading the canon, and in particular reading a novel canon that resembled the one offered above, would, it was hoped, develop taste and judgment in the reader; it would teach the reader to love virtue and despise vice; and to value propriety in discourse, including the central novelistic tenets of probability, realism, and genius. Familiarity with the canon was a key to unlocking social, economic, and cultural possibilities which were not available in the "cultural provinces" of Scotland, Ireland, and the American colonies (Miller 1–2).

The theory of the novel that emerged during the Romantic era had far-reaching effects. The novel histories, theories, and canons which developed at this time established a literary pedigree for the novel, formalized the importance of probability and realism as critical criteria for judging the novel, and formulated a canon based on belletristic principles of taste and judgment. These concepts remained in force for much of the nineteenth century. Victorian novel critics such as David Masson would develop their own histories of the genre established on the principles delineated during the romantic era. Masson in particular was aware of the belletristic roots of Victorian novel criticism. In his inaugural lecture as the Regius Professor of Rhetoric and *Belles Lettres* at the University of Edinburgh, a position first filled by Hugh Blair, Masson directly addresses the relationship of *belles lettres* to literature, calling *belles lettres* "the study of literature as a fine art" (Masson 241). By the end of the nineteenth century, George Saintsbury, who served as Regius Professor of Rhetoric and *Belles Lettres* at Edinburgh after Masson, would survey the history of British literary criticism and declare that Hugh Blair was the first critic to "[accept] to the full the important truth that 'Rhetoric' in modern times really means 'Criticism'" (Saintsbury 196). The Victorian appropriation of belletristic principles in the development of novel criticism, particularly in the work of scholars and critics like Masson, is thus the subject of the next chapter.

Chapter 6
Belles Lettres and David Masson's Victorian Theory of the Novel[1]

> *It may be that the representation of social reality is, on the whole, the proper business of the Novel; but even in the representation of social reality the spirit may be that of the far-surveying and the sublime.*
>
> David Masson, British Novelists and their Styles

Introduction: Eighteenth-Century Rhetoric in Victorian Criticism

In the introduction to her 1999 dissertation, Lois Agnew writes that the late Victorian aesthetic movement championed by literary figures such as Thomas Carlyle, John Ruskin, William Morris, Matthew Arnold, and Oscar Wilde was rooted in British rhetorical theory of the previous century (Agnew 2–3). Agnew's dissertation demonstrates rhetoric's impact on late Victorian aestheticism, and while she is not primarily concerned with the presence of rhetorical theory in Victorian novel criticism, her assessment of the relationship between late Victorian aesthetics and eighteenth-century British rhetorical theory is a useful place to begin examining the influence of *belles lettres* within Victorian novel criticism. Regarding the influence of eighteenth-century British *belles lettres* rhetoric on late Victorian aesthetic theory, Agnew asserts:

> [T]he basic presumption . . . that the artistic imagination holds the key to revitalizing both the individual and society can be seen as a dominant theme that shapes British rhetorical theory throughout the latter half of the eighteenth century. Moreover, aestheticism's representation of the struggle between individual expression and social constraints has roots that go even further back in the rhetorical tradition. (Agnew 3)

Agnew also argues that *belles lettres* rhetorical theory is part of an effort by late Victorian aesthetes to "define the relationship between the seemingly private act of producing and receiving art and the individual's moral obligation to

---

[1] Portions of this chapter were previously published in "David Masson, Belles Lettres, and a Victorian Theory of the Novel." *Victorian Literature and Culture*, vol. 43, no. 1, 2015, pp. 1–21. These previously published sections are reproduced with permission of Cambridge University Press.

society" (Agnew 3). To put it another way, eighteenth-century rhetorical theory played a crucial role in the Victorian articulation and conceptualization of the tension between ethics and aesthetics, a tension clearly evident throughout the history of the novel in English.

As this study has demonstrated thus far, belletristic rhetorical theory is present throughout the history of the novel in English, beginning with the earliest examples of the genre. Critical assessments of the novel, from Congreve to Johnson to Burney to Reeve, Barbauld, and Scott implemented belletristic rhetorical concepts as foundational elements in their understanding of the genre. The massive popularity and influence of rhetoricians like Hugh Blair ensured that *belles lettres* provided the critical horizon of expectation as multiple histories, theories, and canons of the novel emerged throughout the Romantic era. Through a brief examination of popular Victorian criticism of the novel – accessing both well-known and less familiar critics – this final chapter will identify the presence of belletristic principles in the horizon of expectation found in Victorian assessments of the novel, especially as articulated in the periodical press and within the academy, and specifically within the work of David Masson, a public intellectual, literary critic, and university professor.

Belles Lettres and Victorian Periodical Novel Criticism: Probability, Propriety, and Genius

The previous chapter's examination of romantic-era histories and theories of the novel followed the development of novel theory up to Scott's *Notices Biographical and Critical*, published in 1820 as part of *Ballantyne's Novelist's Library* and published again in 1829 as a single volume. Periodical criticism of the novel in the years following Scott's death in 1832 continued to reveal the presence of belletristic principles in the novelistic horizon of expectation of early Victorian literary culture. But assessing the presence of any specific and consistent critical stance in Victorian criticism is a difficult task. John C. Olmsted rightly observes that any attempt to evaluate Victorian criticism of the novel is problematic:

> [Victorian periodical criticism is] inconsistent, [and] most of it is deservedly forgotten . . . The reader [of early Victorian novel criticism] finds he must take into account the prejudices of individual reviewers, the political affiliation of the periodical in which a review appears and, all too often in the 1830s, the ties that journals and reviewers had with publishing houses. (Olmsted xiii – xiv)

Another problem in assessing Victorian novel criticism lies in the aggressively non-theoretical stance of many Victorian critics. As Edwin Eigner and George Worth observe, Victorian criticism of the novel "was written by highly intelligent reviewers and essayists ... [most of whom] rather prided themselves on the non-theoretical character of their intellects" (Eigner and Worth 1). The perceived or actual absence of theory in Victorian criticism makes the task of identifying common theoretical concerns and systematic approaches a difficult proposition.

Yet there is a common theoretical component in much Victorian criticism, and these theoretical leanings are often explicitly beholden to belletristic rhetorical principles. For example, in an 1840 review of *The Dowager* published in *The Athenaeum*, Catherine Gore begins by pointing out the presence of "canons of criticism" which include "the prevailing state of education, the current acquaintance with rhetoric, with the principles of the sublime and beautiful, or, in one word, with the science and the art of composition" (Gore 899). References to rhetoric, to sublimity and beauty, and to the art of composition all specifically recall belletristic concerns with aesthetics and the ability to both produce and judge written discourse. Victorian novel criticism such as this reveals a horizon of expectation predicated on a belletristic critical foundation, particularly regarding the *belles lettres* trinity of probability, propriety, and genius.

Harriet Martineau's 1833 *Tait's Magazine* essay, "Achievements of the Genius of Scott," is an excellent place to begin examining the presence of *belles lettres* rhetorical theory in Victorian novel criticism: Scott's place as the preeminent novelist of the early nineteenth century ensured that his works would be used as a basis of comparison for the fiction produced throughout the Victorian era. In her examination of the impact of Scott's fiction, Martineau restates the primary principles of romantic-era novel theory: by repeatedly invoking the well-known belletristic concerns for taste, moral purpose, propriety, verisimilitude, and genius, she builds a case for the monumental import of Scott's fiction.

While Martineau's essay leans toward the hagiographic in its unfiltered admiration for Scott's achievements, it is nonetheless an important critical statement because of the way it develops a theory of the novel which simultaneously looks back to the theorization of the novel, which took place during the Romantic era, and forecasts the emergence of Victorian novelists and critics who would share Martineau's views on what fiction could and should become. Martineau praises Scott for demonstrating the full potential of novel-writing: she admires him for the moral, though un-didactic, nature of his fiction, for his ability to gently satirize and expose human folly and vice, and for the good-natured kindliness which Martineau finds infused throughout the entirety of Scott's catalog (Martineau 445). Martineau contextualizes Scott's effect on the morality of his readers by claiming that Scott's fiction has had a greater impact than the combined influence of all the clergy, all the teachers at all the universities, and all contemporary philosophers (Martineau 445–446), a statement which recalls Anna Laetitia Barbauld's well-known claims about the power of popular novels. Scott's influence is due to the nature of the novel as a genre: Martineau, echoing the novel theorists of the Romantic era – including Scott – argues that the reading public is much more likely to respond to lessons exemplified in fiction than to preaching and teaching.

Martineau resists specificity in her praise for Scott, but the belletristic influence on her critical paradigm is difficult to miss. Apart from the moral purpose of Scott's fiction, Martineau claims that Scott's fiction has "implanted or nourished pure tastes . . . in a thousand homes" (Martineau 447). Furthermore, the "pure tastes" fostered through Scott's fiction have been "gratified by the creations of his genius" (Martineau 448). Martineau's assessment is thoroughly belletristic: moral purpose, taste, and genius are central tenets of *belles lettres*. The idea of verisimilitude is also clearly present in Martineau's argument that one of Scott's greatest achievements is "the introduction of the conception of nature, as existing and following out its own growth in an atmosphere of convention" (Martineau 448). Scott, Martineau argues, presents a realistic version of the natural world; furthermore, Martineau praises Scott's ability to portray all classes, from the rural laborer to the royal family, in a realistic, though often charitable light (Martineau 449). The only problem with Scott's attention to the true representation of all classes, Martineau argues, is his tendency to "throw the gloss of romance" over his presentation of the upper classes and their various vices and shortcomings (Martineau 449). Yet this fault is easily forgiven, if not entirely overlooked, because of the far-reaching impact of Scott's artistry. In her praise for Scott's attention to the moral purpose of his fiction, in his development of appropriate taste, in his purposeful deployment of verisimilitude to generate sympathy between the classes, and – above all – in her oft-repeated invocation of his genius, Martineau's essay clearly articulates the belletristic critical assessment of fiction as a vehicle for both aesthetic and moral concerns.

Such statements of belletristic-infused expectations for novels are clearly present across a large range of periodical criticism throughout the 1830s. Two years before Martineau committed her admiration for Scott to the page, William Hazlitt's review of *Caleb Williams* praises William Godwin's realistic portrayal of the title character's "ordinary and unformed sentiments" and the "individuality and contrast in the characters" (Hazlitt 144). Hazlitt continues, noting that even Godwin's political opponents "were disposed to forgive the author's paradoxes for the truth of imitation with which he had depicted prevailing passions" (Hazlitt 145). And while Hazlitt gives a great deal of credit to Godwin's genius, *Fraser's Magazine* editor William Maginn challenges the genius of Edward Bulwer-Lytton and similar authors. In Maginn's review of Bulwer-Lytton's *The Disowned*, the issue of genius is obliquely referenced when Maginn condemns the popularity of "successful mediocrity" (Maginn 509). Maginn forcefully asserts that of "[m]ediocritists there are always enough and too many, and if they receive encouragement they will overrun the field of fame, and exclude their betters from the arena" (Maginn 509–510). Near the end of the essay, Maginn explicitly references genius as he defends his censure of Bulwer-Lytton by calling on the principle of genius, asserting that "Genius is a rule to itself" (Maginn 514), a rule which apparently excludes Bulwer-Lytton and other authors of contemptible fashionable novels.

While probability – typically located in a novel's verisimilitude – and genius are relatively straightforward concepts, propriety is perhaps much more difficult to locate. Yet propriety is a crucial element in the pre- and early Victorian periodical novel criticism. Propriety is applied in two ways during this time. In the first instance, propriety is applied to the actual execution of the narrative, to the author's ability to render artfully the probable and realistic action, setting, and characters of a novel. In the second instance, propriety is applied to the appropriateness of the subject matter to the genre and often (though not always) functions as a measure of the moral suitability of the text.

Thus, when Maginn lambastes Edward Bulwer-Lytton's *The Disowned*, Maginn addresses propriety in both the execution and appropriateness of the novel when he asserts that readers of Edward Bulwer-Lytton's *The Disowned* found the novel "to be absolutely offensive to good taste" (Maginn 511). Maginn finds fault in Bulwer-Lytton's failure to tell his story well: "[e]very thing is . . . disjointed, and seemingly out of place—all the *dramatis personae* are, as it were, brought together by accident, and by accident too most of them are disposed of" (Maginn 514). Maginn's sense of novelistic propriety is also offended by the rejection of the middle-class in the fashionable novel: "it is a favourite notion with our fashionable novelists, to sacrifice the middle classes equally to the lowest and highest . . . a work, in fact, which is peculiarly calculated for the vulgar of all degrees" (Maginn 515). Maginn is asserting that novelistic propriety is directly associated with a horizon of readerly expectation: the narrative must be well executed and must not transgress the expectations of the reading audience by rejecting those expectations – in this instance, by rejecting the sympathy for the middle classes often associated with the novel genre.

While propriety was often conflated with moral purpose, critics frequently made fine distinctions between novels with immoral subject matter and novels which violated the principles of novelistic propriety by failing to meet reader expectations concerning the execution of the narrative. In Dinah Mulock Craik's April 1861 *MacMillan's* review of George Eliot's *The Mill on the Floss*, for example, Craik clearly draws a distinction between merely "impure and immoral books" and works like Eliot's, which Craik considered artistically pure, yet in violation of her understanding of propriety (Craik 442). Craik invokes all three tenets of belletristic criticism in her appreciation of *The Mill on the Floss*. Craik first praises the novel's sense of the probable and compositional propriety, found in Eliot's ability to "[amalgamate] real materials into a foreplanned ideal scheme; the power of selection, able to distinguish at once the fit and the unfit, choosing the one and rejecting the other, so as to make every part not only complete as to itself, but as to its relation to a well-balanced whole" (Craik 443). Craik goes on to invoke the criteria of genius, asserting that the author of *The Mill on the Floss* is "one of the truest *artists*, in the highest sense, of this or any age" (Craik 443).

Yet Craik finds fault on the grounds of propriety, because the novel, for all its perfection, fails to meet her readerly expectations concerning novels. Craik finds it exceptionally difficult to articulate just what those expectations are: she clarifies that she is not questioning "literary morality,—the external morality which . . . our modern reading public both expects and exacts and here undoubtedly finds" (Craik 443). Craik instead ventures to criticize the novel for failing to meet an undefined expectation of artistic or aesthetic propriety, particularly regarding the novel's tragic conclusion.

Several years earlier, Eliot herself invoked a sense of novelistic propriety similar to Craik's in "Silly Novels by Lady Novelists," her well-known 1856 essay published in the *Westminster Review*. Eliot's entire critique of the sort of light, fashionable fiction that she herself would never write is predicated on her sense of propriety concerning her expectations for the genre. Eliot is speaking for an imagined reading public, with a very specific horizon of expectation for their fiction, as evidenced in Eliot's repeated invocation of "we" instead of "I." Eliot, though, inverts the use of propriety, arguing that the propriety which governs expectations for such novels is unfortunately clichéd and tired. Speaking of the heroines of such novels, Eliot invokes and inverts the belletristic concept of genius as she wryly remarks that "[w]e [the readers] are assured, again and again, that she had a remarkably original mind, that she was a genius, and 'conscious of her originality'" (Eliot, "Silly Novels" 444).

Eliot clearly articulates her own conception of novelistic propriety in "The Natural History of German Life," her essay July 1856 essay published in the *Westminster Review*. As part of an ongoing critical argument about novels of the "real" versus those of the "ideal" schools, Eliot writes a forceful argument for the moral necessity of writing real, rather than ideal, novels. Eliot asserts that most middle- and upper-class conceptions of lower-class life are idyllic, due to the lingering effects of British romanticism. Idealism, in novels which purport to present common people realistically, is designated a "grave evil" by Eliot (Eliot, "Natural History" 54). Echoing Martineau's arguments about Walter Scott's literary and social contributions, Eliot argues that accurate portrayals of the lower classes do more "toward[s] linking the higher classes with the lower, towards obliterating the vulgarity of exclusiveness, than by hundreds of sermons and philosophical dissertations" (Eliot, "Natural History" 54).

As many other Victorian critics do, Eliot links her arguments about the real and ideal in fiction with a conception of the moral function of novels. But Eliot's ideas about moral fiction are unconcerned with morality or didacticism in a traditional sense. Instead, Eliot asserts that the moral function of literature lies in the ability of novels to generate sympathy for people outside the normal range of the reader's experience through the accurate – though fictional – portrayal of life as it truly exists. Eliot argues that this is an essential part of participating in humanity:

> The thing for mankind to know is, not what are the motives and influences which the moralist thinks *ought* to act on the labourer or the artisan, but what are the motives and influences which *do* act on him. We want to be taught to feel . . . for the peasant in all his coarse apathy, and the artisan in all his suspicious selfishness. (Eliot, "Natural History" 54–55)

Thus, the fiction of the ideal school does a serious disservice to its readers: by presenting a wider scope of life in an idyllic light, the reader remains uninformed about life beyond their own range of experience and thus the sympathy for others which is at the center Eliot's conception of moral fiction is never roused. Eliot advocates for a fiction which educates the reader's taste (a primary concern of *belles lettres* rhetoric) to be sensitive to the subjectivity of the characters represented in realistic novels. Eliot argues that this attunement to casuistic, individual circumstances encourages the development of true moral sympathy, the primary purpose and function of good art. Eliot's conclusions resonate with belletristic concerns: the only way for novelists to foster moral sympathy in their readers is through adherence to a strict sense of probability and verisimilitude.

But Eliot's novel criticism does not neglect the question of novelistic propriety. Instead, Eliot begins to conflate probability with propriety. In "Silly Novels by Lady Novelists," Eliot attacks the questionable probability of "silly" novels. Eliot's criticism of the readerly expectations for such novels draws a clever distinction between reader expectations – what readers expect will probably happen in the novel's plot – and probability, which deals with the novel's ability to render the fictional materials of the novel in a probable and realistic fashion. Eliot simultaneously criticizes both the propriety and probability of silly novels when she makes note of the "vacillating syntax and improbable incident" common to the genre.

"The Natural History of German Life" and "Silly Novels by Lady Novelists" are important critical statements, not only for Eliot's forceful advancement of realistic fiction, but also for the conflation of two crucial components of belletristic rhetorical criticism. Eliot's insistence that realism is the only way for novelists to develop the moral sensibilities of their readers merges probability with propriety. If the highest aspiration of the novelist is to foster sympathy in readers across social, economic, and class lines, and if an intensely focused realism is the best – if not the only – way for the novelist to achieve such an aspiration, then realism – a concept grounded in a belletristic emphasis on probability and verisimilitude – *is* the measure of novelistic propriety.

Of course, the argument can be made that simply identifying the multitude of instances in which a Victorian critic uses a belletristic critical term is not the same as definitively demonstrating that *belles lettres* rhetorical criticism is synonymous with Victorian novel criticism. But my argument in this study – and specifically in this chapter – is that *belles lettres* rhetorical theory and practice of the eighteenth century provided the critical framework for Victorian discussions of the genre. The wide influence of b*elles lettres* rhetoric in eighteenth- and nineteenth-century British literary culture created a horizon of expectation within novel reading audiences, as well as developed and dispersed the critical terminology – found in terms such as taste, probability, propriety, genius, and moral purpose – which became central to any Victorian discussion of novels. An extended close examination of the work of David Masson – magazine editor, literary critic, and university professor – demonstrates the extent to which the theoretical stance of an influential public voice within Victorian literary culture was formed by the *belles lettres* tradition.

Though Masson served for half a century as a university professor at both University College, London and the University of Edinburgh, the choice to focus on Masson is due in large part to Masson's status as a critic outside the academy: his six volume Milton biography[2], along with his production as a critic within the periodical press and his role as the first editor of *Macmillan's Magazine* make Masson a major figure in Victorian literary criticism. While currently there is no readily available complete bibliography of Masson's work[3], his scholarly and critical output was immense: Masson published twenty-six books of biography, history, and literary criticism and the *Dictionary of Literary Biography* lists a selected bibliography of Masson's periodical writing that

---

[2] Masson's Milton biography is still considered to be one of the foundational texts in Milton studies (Wilson).

[3] Partial bibliographies of Masson's work exist, primarily as addendums to biographical dictionary entries such as Masson's entry in the *Dictionary of Literary Biography*. Mary Plincke's 1952 dissertation at the University of London, *David Masson: A Bibliography*, is an intriguing title; however, at this time I have been unable to view either of the two existing copies.

includes over 100 articles published in *Macmillan's, Fraser's, The North British Review, The British Quarterly Review, The Edinburgh Review,* and a host of other periodicals (Wilson).

Masson was exceptionally well-respected: Thomas Carlyle, for example, described Masson as "a man of truly superior qualities, calculated at once to secure success in his undertakings, and the love of his fellow-creatures by the way. A man of many attainments in scholarship and literature; and with a natural fund of intelligence, delicate, strong, and deep, such as belongs to very few" (Carlyle qtd. in Wilson). In Masson's *Dictionary of Literary Biography* entry, Hugh Wilson asserts that due to his reputation and corpus, "Masson occupies a rank only slightly below that of the greatest Victorians" (Wilson). In their collection of literary biographies, *British Authors of the Nineteenth Century*, Stanley J. Kunitz and Howard Haycraft assert Masson's importance as a standard authority on Milton, Goldsmith, and De Quincey and characterize him as "a writer of good judgment and sound sense" (Kunitz and Haycraft 423). Masson, then, was a well-regarded critic and scholar whose production in the periodical press ranks him as one of the most productive and influential critics of the latter half of the nineteenth century.

The breadth and volume of Masson's corpus render a comprehensive treatment unfeasible in this space[4]. Instead, I will examine his 1859 book, *British Novelists and their Styles*, published while Masson taught at University College, London; perform a close reading of his 1851 *North British Review* article defending Dickens' *David Copperfield* as representative of his periodical criticism; and conclude with a survey of his lectures at the University of Edinburgh, which he presented every term from 1865 until his retirement in 1890.

David Masson's Victorian Theory of the Novel: *British Novelists and their Styles*

Masson provides one of the most extensive and fully realized iterations of novel theory to emerge during the Victorian era. Masson's theory of the novel as presented in *British Novelists* (1859) is a thorough, meticulous, and systematic examination of the genre: the novel is defined, historicized, theorized, and criticized for more than three hundred pages. Masson's theory is clearly indebted to the belletristic tradition of the previous century, yet it is consciously situated within the cultural and aesthetic concerns of mid-century Victorian literary culture. Specifically, Masson frames his theory of the novel through a reading of literary history which focuses on a particularly belletristic triumvirate of

---

[4] Masson has received relatively little scholarly attention; extended treatments of his life and work are primarily found in a few graduate theses and dissertations. See Appendix 1 for a brief bibliography of existing Masson materials.

realism, moral purpose, and sublimity as the key defining characteristics of the genre.

Masson begins by defining the novel in relation to other literary genres. The novel is situated within a taxonomy of imaginative literature; Masson asserts that the novel is a species of poetry and is in fact the "prose counterpart to Narrative Poetry" (*British Novelists* 12). Furthermore, the novel can aspire to true greatness: "the novel, at its highest, is a prose epic" (12). For Masson, the association of the novel with the epic is crucial: linking the novel with the epic provides a framework for historicizing the novel, as well as offering a heuristic for understanding future developments of the genre (12–13). Masson defends the comparison of "one of our thousand-and-one stories of society in Mayfair, and Homer's old story of the wanderings of Ulysses" by citing German scholar Christian Charles Josiah Bunsen's assertion that only the prose fiction of the previous three centuries which can be regarded as epic is still remembered (13). Indeed, Vincent B. Sherry cites Masson when he argues that Joyce's *Ulysses* is the culmination of the blending of the epic and novel forms in "a thickening mixture of ethics and aesthetics" (Sherry 15). In the correct context, Masson argues that not only are novels always comparable to epic poetry, but that such a comparison is a necessary component in understanding the genre:

> In short, if we think only of good novels in connection with good narrative poems, throwing equally out of sight what is inferior in both departments, the association of the Novel with the Epic will not seem so much amiss. At all events, in tracing the history of a Novel, there will be some advantage in recollecting the association. The phases through which the Novel has passed will be found to be not unlike those through which Narrative Poetry has passed; and, in any particular country, the Prose Fiction of a period will be found to exhibit the characteristics seen also in the contemporary Narrative Poetry. (Masson, *British Novelists* 14–15)

Masson's sustained association of the novel with the epic demonstrates two of the most salient features of his theory of the novel: the importance of historical contextualization and the necessity of literary situatedness.

Masson continues to defend his definition, arriving at the conclusion that one of the primary differences between narrative prose and narrative verse is the suitability of prose for humor and the presentation of everyday life and circumstance (*British Novelists* 24–27). This is a crucial point: Masson's assertions concerning the commonplace and everyday as novelistic subject matter are hardly original; however, Masson's identification of the novel as a genre intrinsically and uniquely suited to the task of providing a realistic representation of everyday life moves beyond a typical invocation of the ordinary as novelistic subject matter. Rather than viewing the commonplace and ordinary as the subject matter most frequently chosen by novelists, Masson implicitly argues the reverse: the selection of prose fiction as a mode of literary discourse necessarily leads to the selection of everyday and ordinary subjects. At times, Masson's arguments seem to anticipate a Bakhtinian sense of the novel's capacious nature, asserting that the novel is better suited to a wide range of possibilities: apart from the intrinsic presentation of everyday life and actions, novels are better at depicting historic narratives (*British Novelists* 26), and furthermore, novels are superior in eliciting "efficient action in existing social controversy" (*British Novelists* 27).

Masson uses the association of the novel with the epic as a way to describe the general thematic territory of the genre, but he follows this discussion with an examination of the importance of a novel's conception: "In a prose romance or novel, as in a narrative or heroic poem, the first or main matter of interest for the critic, is the scheme, the idea, the total meaning, the aim, the impression, the subject" (Masson, *British Novelists* 31). Masson then succinctly sums up the relationship of the novelist to realism, morality, and probability:

> [T]o state the matter differently, the novelist, as the creator of his mimic world, is also its providence; he makes the laws that govern it; he conducts the lines of events to their issue; he winds up all according to his judicial wisdom. It is possible, then, to see how far his laws of moral government are in accordance with those that rule the real course of things . . . In short, the measure of the value of any work of fiction, ultimately and on the whole, is the worth of the speculation, the philosophy, on which it rests, and which has entered into the conception of it. (*British Novelists* 33)

Masson's understanding of realism and morality is exceptionally complex: novelistic realism is not simply located in a novel's mimicry of exterior reality, but is also grounded in the conception of reality determined by the author to be appropriate to the novel's subject and purpose. Realism is thus not only an exterior criterion, but is also a matter of internal consistency; moral purpose is much more than a simple application of existing social mores to a narrative, but is also a measure of the novelist's ability to successfully execute the moral framework chosen for the novel[5] (*British Novelists* 31 – 33).

---

[5] In this regard, Masson seems to presage Henry James' assertion in his 1884 article, "The Art of Fiction," that in novels, "the measure of reality is very difficult to fix" and "reality [is] so coloured by the author's vision" (James 193). James goes on to argue, in terms similar to Masson's critical language, that *Treasure Island* is a good novel primarily because Stevenson succeeds in achieving the full realization of his concept, while by

Masson's belletristic tendencies emerge most clearly as he homes in on probability as a primary characteristic in the horizon of expectation for novels. Masson states that "improbability of an incident may well be its [a novel's] condemnation" and further, a reader's "resentment of improbability of incident is a wholesome critical feeling" (Masson, *British Novelists* 35). Probability, in fact, is the dividing line between the novel and romance. Romances typically contain incidents of lower probability than novels and thus "where we find a certain degree of ideality of incident, we call the work a Romance" (*British Novelists* 36). The belletristic concern for moral content is also present in Masson's theory of the novel: Masson draws the line between good and great literature at the novelist's ability to "contrive . . . to give us valuable matter over and above the mere fiction of the story" (*British Novelists* 41). Probability and virtue – central tenets in the *belles lettres* tradition – are core concepts in Masson's novel theory.

After establishing the literary context for the novel within the novel's relationship to the epic, Masson moves on to develop the historical position of the novel. Like his Romantic-era predecessors – Beattie, Reeve, Moore, Dunlop, Barbauld, and Scott – much of Masson's theory is developed along historical lines, and a great deal of *British Novelists* is devoted to articulating the history of the genre. Masson finds the origins of both varieties of prose fiction – the novel and the romance – in the work of ancient Greek and Roman writers, including Heliodorus, Apuleius, Longus, and Petronius. Masson, however, is not convinced that these are truly novels, or even good examples of prose fiction: he declares that "the general impression which they leave is stifling, and even appalling" (*British Novelists* 46), though he does praise them for the "increased liberty of speech and action they give to women" and for "illustrating the state of society towards the close of the Roman empire." Masson then pushes through a few Byzantine and medieval examples, including the *Lives of Saints*. Masson argues that the broader emergence of prose fiction has linguistic roots: as vernacular languages expanded their purview, prose fiction found a wider audience (Masson, *British Novelists* 45–50).

Masson's history of the novel continues to follow a now-familiar path: Masson cites Boccacio, Rabelais, D'Urfé, *Amadis de Gaul*, various Spanish picaresque novels, and finally Cervantes' *Don Quixote* as the Renaissance forebears of the prose fiction proto-novels of the seventeenth century (*British Novelists* 52–55). The history of English prose fiction includes the Arthurian corpus in Geoffrey of Monmouth and Malory and expands to the chap-book legends of Robin Hood, Prester John, and Faustus, before More's *Utopia*, Bacon's *Atlantis*, Sidney's

---

comparison, Edmond de Goncourt's *Chérie* is a bad novel because it "fails deplorably" in achieving de Goncourt's novelistic project (203).

Arcadia, and Bunyan's *Pilgrim's Progress* round out the pre-seventeenth century survey of English prose fiction (*British Novelists* 55–85). This recitation of the novel's pedigree has much the same effect in Masson's text as it does in the Romantic-era novel histories examined in the previous chapter: Masson establishes a historical context for situating the novel as a legitimate form of literature worthy of further critical study and examination. Linking the novel to a respectable literary history is a belletristic endeavor: *belles lettres* rhetoric emphasized the importance of studying approved models in the development of taste, and novels – even in mid-century Victorian culture – were often seen as morally suspect. A respectable literary lineage could alleviate some of those concerns.

Masson weaves belletristic rhetorical concerns throughout his literary and historical assessment of the novel. In the discussion of eighteenth-century British novels, Masson observes that fiction of the period is admirable not only for the realistic depictions of everyday life and firm moral purpose, but also for the stylistic excellence of the novels. Masson argues that in eighteenth-century novels, prose fiction – for the first time in literary history – exceeds poetry in conception of purpose and execution of design. Masson characterizes eighteenth-century poetry as mostly pedestrian, with the notable exceptions of Pope and Thomson. Eighteenth-century prose, though, is described as more consistently excellent, both in design and execution, than at any other time in the history of British literature:

> It [the eighteenth century] is clearly an age in which Prose was, on the whole, the more congenial, and in which the most important and effective work of the British mind . . . devolved on Prose naturally, and was shared in by Verse chiefly because Verse had come sorely down in the world . . . [H]as not Prose the evident advantage, even in the finer and subtler exercises of mind? (Masson, *British Novelists* 96)

The novel, in Masson's estimation, reached the height of its potential in the eighteenth century as Defoe, Richardson, and Fielding fused realism, moral purpose, and excellence in narrative design and execution into a species of prose fiction which exceeded both contemporary poetry and almost all previous prose fiction in English.

Perhaps Masson's most clearly belletristic assessment of the novel comes on the final page of the *British Novelists*. As Masson summarizes the evidence of genius in novel writing, he invokes the concept most important in the *belles lettres* tradition: the sublime. Masson reiterates that novels can – and sometimes do – rise to the same lofty heights as great poetry, despite the novel's typical concern with the commonplace and everyday: "It may be that the representation of social reality is, on the whole, the proper business of the Novel; but even in the representation of social reality the spirit may be that of the far-surveying and the sublime" (*British Novelists* 312). This evocation of the sublime as part of his closing statements on the novel demonstrates the importance of the sublime to Masson's critical project. One conclusion that can certainly be reached is that the eighteenth-century *belles lettres* tradition to which Masson was intellectually indebted[6] was a crucial component in his Victorian criticism of the novel. Belletristic concerns for style, taste, judgment, probability, genius, and moral intent are diffused throughout the body of Masson's criticism, not only his full-length scholarly texts like British *Novelists*, but also in the periodical press and his lectures delivered at the University of Edinburgh.

Masson's *Belles Lettres* Criticism in Practice:
A Defense of Dickens' *David Copperfield*

In their anthology of Victorian criticism, Edwin M. Eigner and George J. Worth observe that novel criticism of the Victorian era was largely divided between supporters of realism and supporters of a more romantic and ideal understanding of how the novel functioned (Eigner and Worth 2–3). Despite the mass popularity of novels from the romantic school throughout the nineteenth century, such novels were often relegated to the literary purgatory of "light literature." Masson confronted this kind of literary high-mindedness in *British Novelists and their Styles*. When Masson describes Charles Dickens as "a novelist of the Ideal or Romantic school" (Masson, *British Novelists* 248), he is referring to contemporary criticism of Dickens which dismissed him as a purveyor of light literature which hardly qualified as art. As Phillip Collins observes, many serious literary critics of the time considered Dickens' work decidedly un-literary: he appealed to the masses, employed broad humor, worked in caricatures, and was overtly moralistic in his tone and approach to social issues. Collins cites the *Saturday Review*, the *Quarterly Review*, and the *Times* as publications which denounced "Dickens and other purveyors of 'light literature'" and further, these publications "classed him [Dickens] as belonging to a Light Literature unworthy of serious discussion" (Collins 13).

To a certain extent, Masson agrees with these views when he states that Dickens is "more light and poetic in his method" (Masson, *British Novelists* 248) when compared to some other novelists[7]. However, Masson is quick to affirm that Dickens' idealized style is a legitimate mode of novelistic discourse. Yet the

---

[6] At the University of Edinburgh, Masson held the Regius Professorship formerly occupied by Hugh Blair.

[7] Specifically, Masson is comparing Dickens and Thackeray but his reading of Dickens' work attempts to defend Dickens' more idealistic concerns against broad criticisms concerning Dickens' romantic tendencies.

necessity of Masson's insistence on the legitimacy of Dickens' lighter poetic tone as a mode of serious novelistic expression indicates an uneasiness with the trans-genre association of novels with more romantic and idealized modes of expression. Masson's defense of Dickens ultimately indicates Masson's indebtedness to the *belles lettres* rhetorical tradition of the eighteenth century. Because of Masson's place as an influential and prolific Victorian critic of the novel, it is important to understand the undervalued contributions of eighteenth-century rhetoric – and specifically belletristic rhetoric – to the development of his novel criticism in the Victorian periodical press.

As described in the examination of Masson's *British Novelists and their Styles*, the intellectual heritage of *belles lettres* is obvious in Masson's criticism of the novel. In his inaugural lecture after assuming the Regius Chair at the University of Edinburgh in 1865, Masson specifically defines *belles lettres* as the study of "literature as a fine art" (Masson, "Inaugural" 241). Later in the lecture, Masson identifies a theory of style[8] as the first and most important component in developing a comprehensive philosophy of literature ("Inaugural" 243). The title of Masson's full-length critical study of the novel, *British Novelists and their Styles*, highlights the importance of style – one of the five classical canons of rhetoric and the canon most dear to belletristic rhetoricians – in Masson's critical work and serves to underscore Masson's background in eighteenth-century Scottish rhetoric and his clear debt to Hugh Blair's development of belletristic rhetorical theory.

Blair's critical stance toward novels has been identified and developed throughout this study, so a few brief comments should suffice to demonstrate how Blair's comments on novels in his *Lectures on Rhetoric and Belles Lettres* resonate when compared to Masson's defense of Dickens. Blair concedes that novels may seem to be an insignificant and sub-literary genre, but in Lecture XXXVII, he admits that the influence of novels cannot be ignored: "any kind of writing . . . that obtains a general currency . . . must demand a particular attention. Its influence is likely to be considerable, both on the morals and taste of a nation" (Blair 420–421). Blair continues to describe novels' potential for positive influence, saying "They [novels] furnish one of the best channels for conveying instruction, for painting human life and manners, for showing the errors into which we are betrayed by our passions, for rendering virtue amiable and vice odious" (Blair 421). In addition, Blair's praise for fiction of a more romantic nature – more fantastic and beyond the "train of common affairs"– is

---

[8] The five classical canons of rhetoric are invention (inventio), arrangement (dispositio), style (elocutio), memory (memoria), and delivery (pronuntiatio). *Belles Lettres* emphasized style above all the other canons while virtually eliminating invention and memory.

expansive. Blair claims that the virtue of this kind of fiction resides in its ability to elevate the mind (Blair 421).

Blair cites Defoe's *Robinson Crusoe* as the most admirable example of the confluence of everyday life, elevation of the imagination, and useful moral instruction in a novel: "No fiction, in any language, was ever better supported than the *Adventures of Robinson Crusoe*. While it is carried on with that appearance of truth and simplicity, which takes a strong hold of the imagination . . . it suggests, at the same time, very useful instruction" (Blair 423). *Tom Jones* is lauded for its humor and Blair approves of Fielding because "the general scope of his stories is favourable to humanity and goodness of heart" (Blair 423). Blair also reserves high praise for Richardson's *Clarissa*, condoning the morality of the novel and the excellence of Richardson's prose style while criticizing his "unfortunate talent" for writing novels of such prodigious length[9] (Blair 424).

Blair thus establishes a two-part criterion for judging the literary value of novels: the *Lectures* are permeated with a concern for linking style and taste with morality and virtue. Blair states that the exercise of taste is "moral and purifying" (Blair 9), and so his development of criteria for judging novels emphasizes the implementation of a clear and concise style which communicates the moral virtues of the novel to the reader. Of primary importance in criticism is a concern for style, which Blair concedes is a difficult concept to define. Simply put, Blair defines style as "the peculiar manner in which a man expresses his conceptions, by means of language" (Blair 99). Good style requires both perspicuity and ornament, but perspicuity – clarity of expression – is paramount. Perspicuity is largely dependent on the use of common, everyday language which is accessible to a broad audience. The importance of perspicuity also outweighs the importance of ornament: without perspicuity, ornamental language is useless and only "puzzle[s], instead of pleasing, the reader" (Blair 100). Correct style is also the only way to express the Sublime in writing, which Blair defines as the intersection of "Boldness and Grandeur in the Thoughts" with "strong exertions of Passion" (Blair 33). The second part of Blair's criteria for judging novels relates to the moral tone of the work in question. In his brief review of the history of prose fiction, romances, and novels, Blair consistently praises works which are "beautified with a very humane morality" while exhibiting contempt for fiction of the "loose and wanton kind" (Blair 421). His praise for Defoe, Richardson, and Fielding largely depends on his admiration of their imaginative powers coupled with their

---

[9] It is interesting to note that in Blair's brief commentary on novels and prose fiction, he identifies Defoe, Richardson, and Fielding as the three most exemplary novelists – the same triumvirate at the center of Ian Watt's seminal *The Rise of the Novel*.

ability to use a style which clearly conveys moral instruction and lessons in virtue.

In Masson's criticism, novelists and novels are evaluated based on a belletristic two-part criterion clearly influenced by Blair: Masson emphasizes the need for a clear and precise style which will allow the reader to easily apprehend the novelist's moral convictions. Masson's defense of Dickens's fiction focuses on style, sublimity, and the power of Dickens' fiction to impart virtue and moral values. Regarding style, Masson describes Dickens' work as "diffuse and luxuriant," a quality which enables his writing to rise "to a keener and wilder song" (Masson, *British Novelists* 240). Masson's characterization of Dickens' work as "lighter and more poetic" is partially grounded in Masson's admiration of the more descriptive passages of Dickens' novels. In his 1851 review of *David Copperfield*, Masson applauds Dickens for being "more capable of the poetic excitement than the majority of his literary contemporaries" (Masson, "Pendennis and Copperfield" 252), an opinion which remained unchanged in 1859 when Masson observed that Dickens "can body forth romantic conceptions of terror or beauty that have arisen in his imagination; he can compose a fantastic fairy piece; he can even succeed in a dream or allegory, where the figures are hardly human" (Masson, *British Novelists* 242).

Masson's observations here clearly coincide with Blair's belletristic concerns: Dickens' ability to develop a sense of hyper-reality while writing novels which (for the most part) deal with everyday life seems to echo Blair's admiration of *Robinson Crusoe*. Blair admires Defoe's ability to combine everyday life with plot elements which take hold of the imagination and suggest higher spiritual importance. Masson observes the same ability in Dickens: while Masson describes Dickens as writing "Novel[s] of English Life and Manners" (Masson, *British Novelists* 238), which display the full range of possibility common to life in England, Masson also affirms Dickens' ability to reach beyond the everyday and common, citing the description of the fateful storm which claims the lives of Steerforth and Ham Peggotty in *David Copperfield* as a scene "which for visual weirdliness, there is nothing comparable in the pages of his rival [Thackeray]" (Masson, *British Novelists* 243). Because Masson is purposely opposing Dickens to Thackeray as examples of the Romantic style versus the Real style in novels, Masson's observations resonate as an affirmation of the poetic presence in Dickens' fiction.

Masson also finds the poetic in Dickens' creation of characters and argues that "as Mr. Dickens' artistic range is thus wider than that of Mr. Thackeray [representative of the "Real" school], so also his style of art is the more elevated" (Masson, "Copperfield and Pendennis" 255). Dickens' characters provide some of the most salient examples of the excellence in style and clear expression of moral virtue (or vice) which was so valued by Masson. Masson goes against some contemporary criticism when he lauds Dickens for creating characters which were so obviously outside the bounds of real life and so far beyond the imaginative capabilities of novelists of the "Real" like Thackeray. Dickens' characters, Masson argues, were never meant to reflect life as it actually is; rather, "[Dickens'] characters are real only thus far, that they are transcendental renderings of certain hints furnished by nature" (Masson, "Copperfield and Pendennis" 256). Masson continues to argue that Dickens' true artistry lies in his ability to build entire characters around the distilled essences of particular vices and virtues and to render these characters so artfully that Micawber or Toots or Uriah Heep are real within the setting of Dickens' novels while simultaneously serving as stand-ins for specific virtues and vices (Masson, *British Novelists* 248–249; 251–252).

Masson also clearly aligns his criticism with Blair and *belles lettres* in his praise of Dickens' forceful expression of moral certitude. Blair's emphasis on the moral quality of great literature is evident throughout the lectures and holds a central place in his brief criticism of novels and novelists. As previously observed, Blair identifies the moral implications in the work of Defoe, Richardson, and Fielding as their most salient and desirable qualities. Similarly, Masson cites Dickens as "singularly aggressive and opinionative" (Masson, *British Novelists* 246) and continues to defend Dickens' overt moralizing against critics who complain that such moralizing detracts from the artistry of Dickens' novels:

> There is scarcely a social question on which he has not touched; and there are few of his novels in which he has not blended the functions of a social and political critic with those of the artist, to a degree detrimental, as many think, to his genius in the latter capacity. For Mr. Dickens's wonderful powers of description are no guarantee for the correctness of his critical judgments . . . And yet how much we owe to Mr. Dickens for this very opinionativeness! With his real shrewdness, his thoughtfulness, his courage, what noble hits he has made! (*British Novelists* 246-247)

Here, Masson diverges from Blair. In Blair's *Lectures*, the artistic success of the novel is tied to its ability to instruct as well as entertain; in Masson's criticism, Dickens' novels succeed artistically *in spite* of their attempts to deliver moral judgments while entertaining.

Masson's continued emphasis on a style which grants the reader easy access to the moral concerns of the novelist, then, is clear evidence of the influence of eighteenth-century belletristic theory in his criticism. In responding to critics opposed to the romantic tendencies in Dickens' novels, Masson deploys a critical understanding of the novel genre which emphasizes the connection between artistry, style, and moral instruction so important to belletristic rhetorical theory. This is not to say that Masson is himself a belletrist; however, it is obvious that Masson's criticism owes a debt to the New Rhetoricians, his intellectual forebears in eighteenth-century rhetorical theory.

David Masson, Novels, and *Belles Lettres* in the Victorian Academy

While Masson's public contributions to Victorian novel criticism are relatively well-documented, his academic work has received almost no attention. Masson's work in the academy deserves further scrutiny, though: for almost half a century, Masson taught rhetoric and literature at University College London and the University of Edinburgh. Masson's role in the history of the novel within the academy is vital. Masson taught one of the earliest courses specifically focused on English-language literature, and his lectures were immensely popular: during his tenure at the University of Edinburgh, his course in Rhetoric and English Literature averaged an enrollment of 183 students and over his twenty-four years at the University of Edinburgh, more than 4,000 students attended his lectures (Masson, *Enrollment*)[10]. An examination of Masson's university lectures, like his periodical criticism and full-length critical studies, clearly demonstrates his indebtedness to *belles lettres* rhetorical theory in the development and exposition of his own critical stance regarding British literature, particularly fiction.

But before discussing Masson's work within the academy, it is important to understand rhetoric's changing place within the Victorian university, and any attempt to understand the impact of rhetorical theory in the Victorian academy is confronted with a difficult fact: rhetoric, as a distinct and robust academic discipline, begins to disappear in the nineteenth century. According to Hayden White, the disappearance of rhetoric during the nineteenth century is directly tied to the emergence of literature as a specialized field of study within the academy. White describes this process as "the progressive derogation of rhetoric in favor of the elevation of poetic to the status of the very principle of literarity, on the one side, and its effective repression, in favor of promoting grammar and logic as the twin components of training in basic literacy, on the other" (White 25). White is arguing that rhetoric – as the study of the nature, function, and production of any mode of discourse – was displaced in the academy by a specialized veneration for "poetic" and artistic modes of discourse. The birth of literature as a distinct subject for academic study, according to

---

[10] Prior to Masson's course, William Edmondstoune Aytoun's course averaged eighty-three students over twenty years (Aytoun, *Enrollment*). In addition, Masson's popularity with his students is evidenced in the various newspaper clippings which announce Masson's public lectures and are slipped into the student lecture notes housed at the University of Edinburgh.

White, sounded the death knell for a centuries-long tradition of rhetorical training and education.

White perhaps overstates the case: the nineteenth century was certainly not the first time that a revision to the purview of rhetoric had taken place, and arguments about the relationship between rhetoric, logic, and grammar have a permanent place in the history of rhetorical theory and pedagogy. But during the Victorian era, rhetoric is, for the first time, subsumed within another discipline. In White's formulation, rhetoric is suppressed by the elevation of literature within the academy; in actuality, rhetoric was not suppressed so much as conscripted by literary studies. Rhetoricians, critics, and literary scholars turned rhetoric's traditional emphasis on the production of discourse toward a focus on the analysis of discourse, and in the process, rhetoric's role in analyzing discourse became circumscribed within literary criticism.

The story of the transition from rhetoric to literary criticism, and the attendant development of English-language literature studies in the academy, has served as something of a counter-historical account: as Robert Crawford observes, "the best-known accounts of the development of university English, such as those by Baldick, Eagleton and Graff, downplay or ignore eighteenth-century Scotland and assume that the middle or concluding years of the nineteenth century in England and America witnessed the subject's birth" (Crawford 2). Yet, as Crawford and others argue, nothing could be further from the truth. As documented by Crawford, Winifred Bryan Horner, Thomas P. Miller, and other scholars, English studies emerged in the rhetoric courses of eighteenth-century Scottish universities and later in the dissenting academies, particularly at London University and King's College, London[11].

One reason that the development of English as a field of study within university rhetoric courses is a less familiar component in disciplinary histories is because, as Horner tells us, "nineteenth-century Scottish rhetoricians . . . usually did not publish their lectures, and, as a result, we are largely ignorant of their important influence" (Horner, "Nineteenth-Century Rhetoric" 365). Yet, as Horner demonstrates in *Nineteenth-Century Scottish Rhetoric: The American Connection*, it is possible to develop a clear understanding of what was taught in nineteenth-century British literature courses in the Scottish universities (Horner, *Nineteenth-Century* 54–164). Horner's archival work at the four ancient Scottish universities reveals the clear presence of British literature as course material in Scottish universities throughout the nineteenth century.

---

[11] Specifically, this concept emerges within Crawford's edited collection *The Scottish Invention of English Literature* (1998), Horner's *Nineteenth-Century Scottish Rhetoric: The American Connection* (1993), and Miller's *The Formation of College English* (1997).

Horner's excellent annotations reveal the belletristic underpinnings of these new courses in English literature. At the University of Glasgow, Horner highlights the work of John Nichol, the first professor of English literature at Glasgow[12]. In his inaugural lecture at the University of Glasgow, Nichol's concern for the improving nature of literature demonstrates a clear debt to belletristic principles:

> The study of our own literature encourages the best sort of patriotism, our pride in our great men. It enlarges our ideas by enabling us to penetrate into their minds and stimulates us to emulate, by setting forth, the qualities which made them great. It takes away our jealousies, by holding up standards, in following which we have need to resign our self-complacency, and waive a little of our individual claims. It tones our rancour down, by showing us the common grounds on which we may meet and shake hands. The study of works which time has allowed to last, is, above all, the best corrective to the impatience of an age ... more noted for critical acuteness than magnanimity (Nichol qtd. in Horner, *Nineteenth-Century* 127)

As Horner observes, Nichol's views are "traditional" in the sense that he espouses a typical mid-century attitude concerning the importance and place of literature studies (Horner, *Nineteenth-Century* 108). These traditional views, though, are belletristic in their foundation: references to "great men" and "standards" and "works which time has allowed to last" all echo a belletristic concern for approved models, fixed notions of taste, and the importance of a canon in the development of correct taste and judgment.

These observations about the general nature of nineteenth-century literature studies at Scottish universities, though, do not necessarily answer any questions about the place of the novel in Scottish university literature courses[13]. But the novel was present in the Scottish universities, and as Paul Bator argues, the novel found its way into university curriculum precisely because of the tradition of belletristic rhetoric in the Scottish universities (Bator 89–91). Bator asserts that the novel found its way into the *belles lettres* rhetorical theories of Adam Smith and Hugh Blair because "the Scottish professors of Rhetoric and Belles Lettres began to view the novel as a utilitarian work of prose fiction that could serve their need for instructive moral examples of taste, sympathy and discreet as well as indiscreet character" (Bator 91). Novels, in other words, could

---

[12] Nichol served as the Regius Professor of English Language and Literature at the University of Glasgow from 1862 – 1889 (Kunitz and Haycraft 471).

[13] Horner makes tantalizing reference to Aberdeen University literature professor Herbert J.C. Grierson's lecture notes, saying that one copy of notes housed at the university contains "a section on the novel" (Horner, *Nineteenth-Century* 164).

be used as a testing ground and delivery system for belletristic principles of taste, judgment, and moral purpose. Bator continues, asserting that as *belles lettres* rhetorical theory shifted emphasis from the production of texts toward the analysis of texts, the prevalence of *belles lettres* rhetoric in the Scottish universities provided "an institutional avenue for the reading and critical consumption of the novel" (Bator 92). As the previous chapter demonstrates, there was a great deal of anxiety about which novels were suitable for study. The result of this anxiety, Bator observes, was a concerted effort on the part of Scottish librarians and rhetoric professors to sanction only "first-tier" fiction (Bator 91).

Bator's scrupulous research demonstrates the presence of the novel in the eighteenth-century Scottish university rhetoric courses: in Adam Smith's lectures at the University of Glasgow, in Blair's lectures at the University of Edinburgh, in James Beattie's lectures at the University of Aberdeen, and in William Barron's lectures at St. Andrews (Bator 92–94). But as Bator observes, these lectures do not treat the novel at any great length and typically end with a warning that readers – particularly young and inexperienced readers – should be very careful about the quality and quantity of novels they consume (Bator 91; 93). Furthermore, Bator warns that it should not be inferred that novels were being "taught" in these courses:

> Since hard curricular evidence or data such as reading lists, syllabi, or detailed assignments is difficult to come by, it should not be said that the novel was actually being 'taught' *per se* in the Scottish universities of the eighteenth century as there was no organized method of introducing novels or novelists; furthermore, the novel was a mixed form of prose fiction and not yet a pure genre by any means. (Bator 92)

Sidestepping any questions about what a "pure genre" might be, Bator's work shows that the novel was considered worthy of academic attention in the Scottish universities at least as early as Smith's lectures in the 1750s. Yet a complete treatment of the novel as a fully accepted genre within the academy was not to come until the nineteenth century.

While Crawford rightly points out the early presence of English literature in the course offerings at all four of the ancient Scottish universities (Crawford 2), for the purpose of expediency, I will focus primarily on the development of English studies at the University of Edinburgh during the latter half of the nineteenth century, particularly regarding the work of David Masson. The substance of Masson's lectures is preserved in seven sets of course lecture notes taken down by students (including *Peter Pan* author, James M. Barrie) and housed at the University of Edinburgh and the National Library of Scotland. Masson never formalized his lectures for publication: the available lecture notes cover seven different courses taught across twenty years, the earliest from 1868 and the latest from 1889. While there are variations among the different versions of the lecture notes (for example, none of the lecture notes give the same name for Masson's course), the lectures demonstrate a remarkable level of uniformity, despite seven different note-takers across two decades.

The presence of rhetorical theory in Masson's lectures is immediately evident, beginning with the earliest existing copies of Masson's lecture notes, taken during the 1868 – 1869 term. Masson describes rhetoric as "the science of literature" (*Notes of English Literature* 4) and Masson's description of how to perform literary criticism reads like an application of stasis theory to literary works (120–131)[14]. The notes from the 1870 – 1871 term include a useful précis which outlines the structure of Masson's lectures: the first half of the course focuses on rhetoric and criticism, especially tropes, figures of speech, and style; the second half of the course provides a history of British literature, classifications of literature, and some application of the rhetorical criticism from the first part of the course (*Notes on Prof. Masson's Lectures*). In the lecture notes taken by James M. Barrie during the 1881 – 1882 term, Masson clearly indicates that rhetorical theory is central to literary criticism: Masson's third and fourth lectures deal with tropes and figures at great length, and he cites several eighteenth- and nineteenth-century rhetoricians (including Kames, Campbell, Blair, Whately, and Bain) as authorities on style, a central focus in Masson's development of criticism (*Rhetoric I & English Literature*). Despite the systematic approach to rhetoric in the service of literary criticism, Masson explicitly rejects the notion that criticism can or should be performed through rote responses to rhetorical conventions. Masson reminds his students that rhetorical theory should not mechanize their approach to criticism, stating that "[l]ike all sound theory, it [rhetorical methodology] helps to guide and correct practice" and furthermore, "No able critic would think of making any mechanical apparatus [to render judgments]" (*Rhetoric I & English Literature*).

For the most part, Masson's approach to literary criticism is driven by a sense of history: in all the lecture notes, Masson devotes a large number of lectures to

---

[14] Stasis theory is an ancient rhetorical concept in which the speaker (or writer) determines the nature of an argument (typically in a legal setting) by asking a series of questions and evaluating the responses. Stasis theory, as developed by Hermagorus, involves four lines of questioning: 1. Conjecture (Did something occur?) 2. Definition (What sort of thing was done?) 3. Qualitative (Was the deed legal?) 4. Translative (Is this the correct venue for trying the case?) (Lanham 93–94). Masson suggests asking the following series of question when approaching a literary text: 1. Is the author a poet? 2. What is his worth as a poet? 3. In what kinds of circumstances does he excel as a poet? 4. In what emotional key is his poetry? 5. In what proportion is his [work] poetic?

developing a notion of the historical periods of British literature (in the lecture notes, Masson seems to delineate five or sometimes six historical periods). Prose fiction – whether under the guise of romance or novel – is mentioned as early as 1688 and is typically divided into two historical periods: pre-1789 and post-1789. The nature of the lecture notes makes it difficult to ascertain exactly how Masson is treating the novels. Several of the sets of lecture notes seem to indicate that Masson had little to say regarding theory or criticism of the novel, and simply listed the authors (and sometimes the works) associated with each period. Even these lists, though, are instructive. Masson's informal canon is clearly influenced by the novel histories and canons of the romantic era examined in the previous chapter. Taking all the lecture notes together, Masson's canon is quite familiar: he includes Defoe, Swift, Richardson, Fielding, Smollett, Johnson, Walpole, Goldsmith, MacKenzie, More, Inchbald, Burney, Austen, Godwin, Beckford, Radcliffe, Scott, Edgeworth, Lytton, Dickens, Thackeray, Eliot, the Bronte sisters, and nominates Dickens and Thackeray as the best contemporary novelists. In the notes from the 1881 – 1882 term taken by George J. Lundsen, Masson claims that there are twenty different varieties of novels, but Lundsen recorded no taxonomy of novel types (*Rhetoric and English Literature*).

But in other copies of the lecture notes, Masson makes critical judgments about novels[15]. In the anonymously recorded notes from the 1878 – 1879 term, Masson names Richardson the "Father of the modern English novel" and praises Defoe's novels as "facsimiles of the real" (*Lectures on English Literature*). Masson also states that "at the end of the previous period [of his divisions of British literary history], the novel of society was an established literature . . . cultivated chiefly by ladies" and of these society novels, "Austen is the chief novelist of the time" (*Lectures on English Literature*)[16]. The notes taken by George J. Lundsen during the 1881 – 1882 term include similar information about the British novel: Radcliffe, Edgeworth, and Austen are named the leading novelists at the turn of the previous century. At this point, Masson reiterates a point about the place of women in the history of the novel that he first offered in *British Novelists and their Styles*, claiming that the novel was a literary fortress long garrisoned by women, and that no male novelists of romantic era, save Godwin, had achieved the same level of artistic success as

---

[15] One amusing moment of what might be Scottish pride (or humor) occurs when Masson declares that Shakespeare was the Sir Walter Scott of his era (*Notes of English Literature*)
[16] At this point in the lecture notes, the note-taker inscrutably notes Masson's assertion concerning novel publishing data, claiming that in 1820, twenty-six novels were published; only ten years later, in 1830, Masson claims that over one hundred were published. This fascinating supposition is provided with no context and no further commentary, though.

their female counterparts (Masson, *British Novelists* 179). In the lecture notes, this idea is truncated, but the presence of Masson's public criticism in his academic work is unmistakable.

Conclusion: Recovering Pre-Twentieth Century Critics of the Novel

In her study of Blair's influence on Victorian education, Linda Ferreira-Buckley suggests that the Victorians should no longer be seen as "simply heirs of the Romantics" and challenges scholars to consider *belles lettres* in future studies of Victorian criticism and culture (Ferreira-Buckley 236). Ferreira-Buckley's study only examines the relationship of Matthew Arnold and John Ruskin to Blair's *Lectures* and she admits that "a period that produced prose as varied as the Victorian era can never be 'represented' by two authors" (Ferreira-Buckley 236). The same idea applies here regarding Masson: the Victorian era is far too rich and complex to allow the relatively brief analysis of one author's work to somehow summarize the critical opinions of the entire period. Masson is certainly not thought of in the same breath as other Victorian critics: as Hugh Wilson observes,

> After World War I, Masson was left behind in undeserved oblivion. Fashionable biographical writers took the more cynical stance epitomized by Lytton Strachey; some critics and academicians turned away from history in the name of "art for art's sake" while others turned toward social and economic history. In literary criticism, the fashionable conservative aestheticism of Henry James and T. S. Eliot, the despairing apolitical nihilism of James Joyce, and the positivism of I. A. Richards fostered a disengagement of writers and scholars from literary history and the kind of ethical concerns that animated Masson. (Wilson)

Masson's fall from favor can be seen as parallel to the disappearance of rhetoric as an activity distinct from the practice of literary criticism: like Masson, rhetoric – and especially belletristic rhetoric – was concerned with historical models, moral purpose, propriety, and the clear delineation of principles of style and perspicuity in discourse. The critical paradigm that emerged in literary studies after World War I, as Wilson observes, had no place for such outmoded concerns. Yet though Masson and his affinity for belletristic rhetorical criticism might seem quaint and naïve when compared to Henry James' prescient criticism or the rigorous aestheticism of the *fin de siècle*, Masson's work is at least as representative of the Victorian approach to literary criticism. Masson's oeuvre demonstrates his firm belief that literature and history were mutually illuminating disciplines and that a thorough understanding of rhetoric was a central component in understanding literature across historical periods.

Curiously though, even Masson occasionally failed to notice the place of *belles lettres* rhetoric in his literary criticism. In Masson's 1856 essay, "Scottish Influence in British Literature,[17]" no mention is made of *belles lettres*, and only the briefest references are made to Blair, Campbell, Reid, Hume, and the other Scottish rhetoricians and philosophers so influential in the development of *belles lettres*, a major component in Masson's intellectual heritage. This ironic omission by a Victorian critic so obviously indebted to the belletristic tradition only highlights the degree to which the important contributions of Scottish *belles lettres* rhetoricians are simultaneously embedded and overlooked in the history and theory of the British novel. Re-establishing and further exploring these connections can only enrich our understanding of the complex literary milieu which surrounded the development of the British novel. David Masson's literary career is an excellent place to start: his clear relationship to *belles lettres* combined with his broad range of intellectual activity – as essayist, editor, critic, and professor – invites a further examination of how the *belles lettres* rhetoric of the eighteenth century undergirded, influenced, and informed the literary criticism and theory of the nineteenth century.

---

[17] Here cited from Masson's 1875 volume, *Wordsworth, Shelley, Keats, and other Essays.*

Chapter 7
Epilogue

"An opportunity of comparing the present school of fiction with the past"
William P. Nimmo, *Episodes of Fiction*

On a brisk November day, after spending the morning and early afternoon conducting my last day of archival research at the University of Edinburgh, my wife and I wandered down Grassmarket into West Bow Street, Edinburgh Castle looming above us. I was looking for antiquarian bookshops: the previous March, my parents had visited Edinburgh and purchased volume one of an 1802 edition of Blair's sermons for me; I hoped for a similarly interesting find. I tried to fully absorb the chaotic atmosphere of the antiquarian bookshops. The mad scatter of books piled on shelves from floor to ceiling, the smell of aged paper and ink and bindings, the intriguing titles of volumes long forgotten by anyone other than ardent collectors and bibliophile scholars, and the sense of potential and possibility around every serpentine corner in every bookshop was intoxicating. I could have spent hours – or days – combing through the potential treasures heaped in each bookshop's endless nooks and crannies.

But I didn't have hours, much less days, and as we stepped into a final book shop, I knew I had to find something now or wait for the next trip to Scotland. I perused quickly and purposefully: the hours spent examining David Masson's lecture notes and enrollment records had convinced me that I wanted to leave Edinburgh with an antiquarian edition of one of Masson's texts. Combing through the casually arranged section of Victorian fiction, I pulled down a volume that was not written by Masson, but intriguing nonetheless. I sat down for a moment or two and examined the beautiful blue and gold binding, the gold leafed pages, and the title of the volume: *Episodes of Fiction*.

I opened the book and read the bibliographic information: the text was published in 1870 by Ballantyne and Company in Edinburgh. The text was an anthology of "choice stories from the great novelists" (Nimmo front matter), and the table of contents contained what I had come to recognize as the usual suspects in the history of the British novel: there were selections from Defoe, Richardson, Fielding, Smollett, Sterne, Walpole, Goldsmith, Beckford, Godwin, MacKenzie, Radcliffe, Charlotte Smith, Mary Shelley, Behn, and Inchbald, as well as others less familiar. What intrigued me about the text was the purpose of the selections. In the introduction, the editor, W.P. Nimmo, claims that the selections were chosen "with the view of illustrating the general character of their style, and presenting the reader with an opportunity of comparing the present school of fiction with the past," and furthermore, "the compiler's object has been to furnish the reader with material for an hour or two of pleasant reading, and the artist with suitable subjects for the exercise of his pencil" (Nimmo vii – viii). Here, then, was a collection of British novelists which harked back to Anna Laetitia Barbauld's *British Novelists Library* or Scott's *Ballantyne's Novelist's Library*; yet unlike Barbauld or Scott, Nimmo had not developed a multi-volume anthology. All these authors were contained within the pages of a single volume.

The belletristic influence on the text was immediately evident: during the latter half of the eighteenth century, the emphasis of *belles lettres* rhetoric on understanding style and developing correct judgments about discourse led to the publication of various anthologies such as Vicesimus Knox's *Elegant Extracts in Prose* (1796), a text which truncated and redacted Blair's lectures at great length and included curtailed versions of some literary texts, including works by Swift and Addison, and historical sketches by Hume and Smollett, to name only a few unwitting contributors. Knox tells the reader that the *Elegant Extracts* are intended to serve as a complete library in one volume ("Advertisement"), and the text ranges broadly across acknowledged examples of compositional excellence from the eighteenth century and beyond. Knox's purpose is clear, and in the advertisement to the eleventh edition (1824), Knox explains:

> It is certain young persons cannot read a book full of so much matter, without great improvement in the English language, together with correct ideas on many pleasing subjects of taste and general literature; and, which is of much higher importance, they cannot fail to imbibe from it, together with an increase of elegant knowledge, the purest principles of virtue and religion. (Knox, "Advertisement")

Knox's text is reductive to a fault, eviscerating rhetorical theory and de-contextualizing literature for the sake of easy consumption and facile comparisons, yet the belletristic purpose is obvious: Knox wants to develop correct usage – compositional propriety – in his readers while providing them with the opportunity to hone their critical judgments. Taste and virtue, two of the core tenets of Blair's rhetoric, are central to the *Extracts*.

And in my hands, I held an example of the same principles applied by a nineteenth-century editor to eighteenth-century British novels, texts which vigorously resist easy anthologizing and reduction. Admittedly, Nimmo's aims are much more modest than Knox's: in the preface, Nimmo hopes that the reader will compare and judge different texts and find the selections worthy of leisure reading (Nimmo vii – viii). The preposterous idea of reducing Richardson's

Clarissa from its sprawling fifteen-hundred pages to a twelve-page anthology selection is hard to articulate, but Nimmo valiantly attempts to do the same for every major novel of the eighteenth century. *Robinson Crusoe* is allowed fifteen pages; *Joseph Andrews* is crammed into eight pages; *Tristram Shandy* and *A Sentimental Journey* are forced to share fourteen pages. Nimmo selects particularly famous or evocative scenes from each text, extracts them from the contextual surroundings of their full-text settings, and offers them up as examples of excellence in novelistic discourse.

Despite the absurdity of this endeavor, such an undertaking is highly instructive. Nimmo's table of contents closely resembles the novel canons of the Romantic era, and his desire to provide examples of excellence in novelistic discourse for the purpose of judging, choosing, and understanding the best British prose fiction is quintessentially belletristic in its outlook. The preface acknowledges that *Episodes of Fiction* also provides readers with the opportunity to compare the best of contemporary fiction – Landon, Thackeray, Bulwer-Lytton, and Dickens are all named but not included in the anthology – with the widely approved and accepted texts of the previous century. This sort of comparison is essentially belletristic: *belles lettres* criticism often hinged on the connection between contemporary examples and the approved models of prior eras.

Nimmo's introduction is a fitting place to conclude this study because of his final caveat. Through the course of this project, I have reached the conclusion that one of the most important – and most often neglected or dismissed – areas of concern for students and scholars who study the history of the British novel is the contemporary criticism which surrounded the novels. The moralistic and non-theoretical nature of most early criticism of British novels may seem archaic and simplistic to scholars attuned to the nuances and complications of critical literary theory as it emerged in the twentieth century. Yet Nimmo, perhaps recognizing the absurdity of his project even as he wrote the preface, points his readers in a useful direction:

> The exigencies of space have compelled him [the editor, Nimmo] to omit several authors from whose works he would gladly have quoted, and to restrict his prefatory notices to the merest enumeration of 'dates' and 'titles.' The reader desirous of further information is referred to Mr. Dunlop's 'History of Fiction,' Mr. Jeaffreson's 'Novels and Novelists,' Miss Kavanaugh's 'English Women of Letters,' Professor Masson's 'British Novelists,' Thackeray's 'Lectures on the English Humorists,' and the admirable memoirs which Sir Walter Scott contributed to 'the Novelist's Library.'

As it concludes, Nimmo's *Episodes of Fiction* directs the reader and student of the British novel to read texts which have been neglected or forgotten in the intervening years, yet the theories and histories of the novel offered by Dunlop, Masson, and Scott were once vibrant, engaging texts which were central to understanding the novel in Victorian Britain. And while twentieth-century and contemporary critics and scholars have all made excellent and important contributions to our understanding of the British novel, perhaps our review of the history and theory of the novel might be well-served by beginning somewhat earlier than Ian Watt's *Rise of the Novel*. Contemporary histories of the novel often seek to be exceptionally expansive in their scope, including texts, authors, and ideas traditionally not associated with the development of the British novel. A similarly broad scope should be applied to *histories* of the novel: we should make room for histories and theories of the novel by Congreve, Blair, Reeve, Beattie, Dunlop, Moore, Barbauld, and Masson because understanding their role in shaping the history of the novel will help us better understand our own.

Appendix A:
A Romantic Era Novel Canon: Counting Novels in Beattie, Reeve, Moore, Barbauld, and Scott

The chart below includes every work of prose fiction or novel mentioned in the six Romantic-era appraisals of the novel reviewed in Chapter 5. Authors / titles in bold appeared in at least three of the six texts and were thus identified as representative of a Romantic Era Novel Canon.

	Romantic Era Novel Canon				Histories of the Novel, 1780 - 1820						
Author	Gender	Nation	Title	Pub. Year	Beattie 1783	Reeve 1785	Moore 1797	Barbauld 1810	Dunlop 1814	Scott 1820	Tot.
More, Thomas	M	English	*Utopia*	1516				X			1
Navarre, Marguerite de	F	French	*Heptaméron*	1558				X			1
Montemayor, Jorge de	M	Portuguese	*Diana*	1559					X		1
Rabelais, François	M	French	*Gargantua and Pantagruel*	1564					X		1
Sidney, Philip	M	English	*Arcadia*	1590				X	X		2
Alemán, Mateo	M	Spanish	*Guzmán de Alfarache*	1599/1604					X		1
Cervantes, Miguel de	M	**Spanish**	***Don Quixote***	1605/1615	X	X	X	X	X	X	6
Croce, Giulio Cesare	M	Italian	*La Vita di Bertoldo*	1606					X		1
Barclay, John	M	**Scottish**	***Argenis***	1621	X			X	X		3
d'Urfé, Honoré	M	French	*L'Astree*	1627					X	X	2
Gomberville, Marin le Roy de	M	French	*Polexandre*	1637					X		1

Author	Sex	Nationality	Title	Year					Total
Scudéry, Madeleine de	F	French	*Ibrahim*	1641				X	1
Costes, Gauthier de	M	French	*Cleopatre*	1648				X	1
Costes, Gauthier de	M	French	*Cassandre*	1650				X	1
Scarron, Paul	**M**	**French**	**Le Roman Comique**	**1651**		X	X	X	**3**
Gomberville, Marin le Roy de	M	French	*Le Jeune Alcidiane*	1651				X	1
Boyle, Roger	M	Irish	*Parthenissa*	1655			X		1
Harrington, James	M	English	*The Commonwealth of Oceana*	1656			X		1
Costes, Gauthier (Calprenède) de	M	French	*Faramond*	1661				X	1
Scudéry, Madeleine de	F	French	*Almahide*	1663				X	1
Furetière, Antoine	M	French	*Le Roman Bourgeois*	1666				X	1
Lafayette (Marie-Madeleine Pioche de La Vergne)	F	French	*Zaïde*	1669		X			1
Bunyan, John	**M**	**English**	**Pilgrim's Progress**	**1678**	X	X		X	**3**
Lafayette (Marie-Madeleine Pioche de La Vergne)	F	French	*Princesse de Cleves*	1678			X	X	2
Behn, Aphra	**F**	**English**	**Oroonoko**	**1688**		X	X	X	**3**
Fénelon, François	M	French	*Telemachus*	1699			X		1
Swift, Jonathan	M	Irish	*Tale of a Tub*	1704	X	X			2
Manley, Delarivier	F	English	*The New Atlantis*	1709			X		1

Appendix A

Author	Sex	Nationality	Title	Year							Total
Arbuthnot, John	M	Scottish	*John Bull*	1712	X						1
Defoe, Daniel	M	English	*Robinson Crusoe*	**1719**	X	X		X	X		4
Swift, Jonathan	M	Irish	*Gulliver's Travels*	1726	X	X					2
Ramsay, Andrew Michael	M	Scottish / French	*Les Voyages de Cyrus*	1727				X			1
Terrasson, Jean	M	French	*Sethos*	1731				X	X		2
Lesage, Alain-René	M	French	*Gil Blas*	**1735**	X	X	X	X		X	5
Marivaux, Pierre de	M	French	*Le Paysan Parvenu*	**1735**		X	X	X			3
Richardson, Samuel	M	English	*Pamela*	**1740**		X			X	X	3
Fielding, Henry	M	English	*Joseph Andrews*	**1742**	X	X	X	X		X	5
Fielding, Henry	M	English	*Jonahan Wild*	1743					X		1
Fielding, Sarah	F	English	*David Simple*	1744				X			1
Marivaux, Pierre de	M	French	*Marianne*	1745		X		X			2
Graffigny, Françoise de	M	French	*Lettres d'une Peruvienne*	1747				X			1
Richardson, Samuel	M	English	*Clarissa*	**1748**	X	X	X	X	X	X	6
Smollett, Tobias	M	Scottish	*Roderick Random*	**1748**	X	X	X		X	X	5
Fielding, Henry	M	English	*Tom Jones*	**1749**		X	X	X	X	X	5
Smollett, Tobias	M	Scottish	*Peregrine Pickle*	**1751**	X	X	X		X	X	5
Haywood, Eliza	F	English	*Betsy Thoughtless*	**1751**		X		X	X		3
Coventry, Francis	M	English	*Pompey the Little*	1751		X		X			2
Fielding, Henry	M	English	*Amelia*	1751		X			X		2
Paltock, Robert	M	English	*Peter Wilkins*	1751		X					1
Lennox, Charlotte	F	Scottish	*The Female Quixote*	1752		X		X			2

Author	Sex	Nationality	Title	Year							Total
Richardson, Samuel	M	English	Sir Charles Grandison	1753	X	X	X	X	X	X	6
Smollett, Tobias	M	Scottish	Ferdinand Count Fathom	1753		X	X			X	3
Haywood, Eliza	F	English	The Invisible Spy	1755		X		X			2
Lennox, Charlotte	F	Scottish	Henrietta	1758		X					1
Johnson, Samuel	M	English	Rasselas	1759	X	X		X		X	4
Hawkesworth, John	M	French	Almoran and Hamet	1761	X	X		X			3
Rousseau, Jean-Jacques	M	French	Julie, ou la nouvelle Héloïse	1761	X		X	X			3
Sheridan, Frances	F	Irish	Sidney Bidulph	1761		X		X	X		3
Beaumont, Anne-Louise Élie de	F	French	Lettres du marquis de Roselle	1761		X					1
Smollett, Tobias	M	Scottish	Sir Lancelot Greaves	1762		X				X	2
Leland, Thomas	M	Irish	Longsword	1762		X					1
Lennox, Charlotte	F	Scottish	Sophia	1762		X					1
Brooke, Frances	F	English	The History of Lady Julia Mandeville	1763		X		X			2
Walpole, Horace	M	English	The Castle of Otranto	1764		X		X	X	X	4
Johnstone, Charles	M	Irish	Chrysal; or, the Adventures of a Guinea	1765		X		X		X	3
Goldsmith, Oliver	M	Irish	The Vicar of Wakefield	1766		X		X		X	3
Scott, Sarah	F	English	The History of Sir George Ellison	1766		X					1
Young, Arthur	M	English	Sir Charles Beaufort	1766		X					1

Appendix A

Sterne, Laurence	M	Irish	*The Life and Opinions of Tristram Shandy, Gentleman*	1767	X	X		X	3
Young, Arthur	M	English	*The Adventures of Emmera*	1767	X				1
Marmontel, Jean-François	M	French	*Bélisaire*	1767		X			1
Sterne, Laurence	M	Irish	*A Sentimental Journey*	1768	X	X		X	3
Mulso, Thomas	M	English	*Callistas; or The Man of Fashion*	1768	X				1
Young, Arthur	M	English	*The Adventures of Miss Lucy Watson*	1768	X				1
Cooper, Maria Susanna	F	English	*The Exemplary Mother*	1769	X				1
Lawrence, Herbert	M	English	*The Life and Adventures of Common Sense*	1769	X				1
Potter, John	M	English	*The History and Adventure of Arthur O'Bradley*	1769	X				1
Smollett, Tobias	M	Scottish	*The Adventures of an Atom*	1769	X				1
Brooke, Henry	M	Irish	*The Fool of Quality*	1770	X	X			2
Jenner, Charles	M	English	*The Placid Man*	1770	X				1
Smollett, Tobias	M	Scottish	*Humphrey Clinker*	1771	X	X	X	X	4
MacKenzie, Henry	M	Scottish	*The Man of Feeling*	1771	X	X		X	3
Griffith, Elizabeth	F	Irish	*Lady Barton*	1771	X				1

Author	Sex	Nationality	Title	Year						Total
Graves, Richard	M	English	The Spiritual Quixote	1773		X	X			2
MacKenzie, Henry	M	Scottish	Man of the World	1773		X			X	2
Goethe, Johann Wolfgang von	M	German	The Sorrows of Young Werther	1774			X			1
MacKenzie, Henry	M	Scottish	Julia de Roubigne	1777			X		X	2
Marmontel, Jean-François	M	French	Les Incas	1777			X			1
Reeve, Clara	**F**	**English**	**The Old English Baron**	**1778**			X	X	X	**3**
Burney, Frances	F	English	Evelina	1778			X	X		2
Graves, Richard	M	English	Columella	1779			X			1
Bage, Robert	M	English	Mount Henneth	1781					X	1
Burney, Frances	F	English	Cecelia	1782			X			1
Bage, Robert	M	English	Barham Downs	1784					X	1
Bage, Robert	M	English	James Wallace	1788					X	1
Bernardin, Jacques-Henri	M	French	Paul et Virginie	1788			X			1
Radcliffe, Ann	F	English	The Castles of Athlin and Dunbayne	1789					X	1
Moore, John	M	Scottish	Zeluco	1789			X			1
Radcliffe, Ann	F	English	A Siciclian Romance	1790					X	1
Radcliffe, Ann	**F**	**English**	**The Romance of the Forest**	**1791**			X	X	X	**3**
Inchbald, Elizabeth	F	English	A Simple Story	1791			X			1
Smith, Charlotte Turner	F	English	The Old Manor House	1793			X			1

Appendix A

Radcliffe, Ann	F	English	*The Mysteries of Udolpho*	1794				X	X	X	3
Godwin, William	M	English	*Things as They Are; or, The Adventures of Caleb Williams*	1794					X		1
Cumberland, Richard	M	English	*Henry*	1795						X	1
Bage, Robert	M	English	*Man as He is Not*	1796				X			1
Radcliffe, Ann	F	English	*The Italian*	1797					X	X	2
Godwin, William	M	English	*St. Leon: A Tale of the Sixtennth Century*	1799					X		1
Edgeworth, Maria	F	Irish	*Belinda*	1801				X			1
Male Authors	79		Total Novels:	16	55	11	59	39	33	
Female Authors	30									

Appendix B:
Scholarly Studies of David Masson

Recent scholarship has begun to pay more attention to the work of David Masson, and Masson appears in several studies and anthologies covering Victorian literary criticism, particularly regarding periodical criticism. Extended scholarly studies, though, are few and far between, and Masson's work is typically dismissed or ignored by most novel historians and theorists. Below is a brief bibliography which covers extended treatments of Masson's life and work. Most of these titles are only available at the institution where the dissertation or thesis was written, though McMurtry's *English Language, English Literature* and Flora Masson's *Victorians All* are more widely available and do appear in this project. Masson is often included in anthologies of nineteenth-century or Victorian literary criticism; however, these appearances rarely provide any secondary insight into Masson's critical paradigm and most often simply present his criticism with little specific contextualization. Finally, Masson's impact as an academic is difficult to explore since access to Masson's university lectures is limited to the archives at the University of Edinburgh and the National Library of Scotland

Brief Bibliography of David Masson Scholarship:

Adams, Michael Wayne. *David Masson: A Study of his Literary Criticism*. Thesis. Austin: University of Texas, 1973.

Carré, Muriel and Christiane d'Haussy. *David Masson in his Times*. Thesis. University of Paris – Est Créteil Val de Marne, 1992.

Hertz, A.L. *Macmillan's Magazine under David Masson: 1859 – 1867*. Thesis. London: British Library, 1982.

Littleton, J.M. *David Masson as Biographer and Critic*. Thesis. University of London, 1974.

Masson, Flora. *Victorians All*. Port Washington, NY: Kennikat Press, 1970.

McMurtry, Jo. *English Language, English Literature: The Creation of an Academic Discipline*. Hamden, Connecticut: Archon Books, 1985.

Plincke, Eveline Mary. *David Masson: A Bibliography*. Diss. University of London, 1952.

Bibliography

Primary Texts

Aristotle. "from *Rhetoric.*" *The Rhetorical Tradition: Readings from Classical Times to the Present*, edited by Patricia Bizzell and Bruce Herzberg. Bedford/St. Martin's, 2001, pp. 179-241.

Austen, Jane. *Northanger Abbey,* edited by Marilyn Gaull, Pearson/Longman, 2005.

Aytoun, William Edmondstoune. *University of Edinburgh Enrollment Book.* 1845 – 1865. MS Da 35 RHE 1. University of Edinburgh Library, Edinburgh.

Barbauld, Anna Letitia. "On Female Studies." (1825). *English Romantic Writers.* edited by David Perkins, Thomson Wadsworth, 1995, pp. 41-43.

___ . "On the Origin and Progress of Novel-Writing." *The British Novelists.* 2nd ed. Vol. 1. London: J. Rivington, et al., 1820.

Beattie, James. "On Fable and Romance." *Dissertations Moral and Critical.* London, 1783.

Behn, Aphra. *Oroonoko,* edited by Joanna Lipking, W.W. Norton, 1997.

Blair, Hugh. [*Lectures on Rhetoric and Belles Lettres*]. 1779. EUL Gen. 1990. Vol. II. University of Edinburgh Library, Edinburgh.

___ . *Lectures on Rhetoric and Belles Lettres.* edited by Linda Ferreira-Buckley and S. Michael Halloran, Southern Illinois University Press, 2005.

Bulwer-Lytton, Edward. "On Art in Fiction." *Victorian Criticism of the Novel,* edited by Edwin M. Eigner and George J. Worth, Cambridge University Press, 1985, pp. 22-39.

Burke, Edmund. *A Philosophical Inquiry into the Origin of Our Ideas of the Sublime and Beautiful.* Penguin, 2004.

Burney, Frances. *Evelina: or, A Young Lady's Entrance to the World.* 2nd Ed. London, L. Townes, 1779.

Campbell, George. *The Philosophy of Rhetoric,* Edinburgh, 1776.

Collins, Wilkie. *The Moonstone.* edited by Joy Connolly, Barnes & Noble Classics, 2005.

Congreve, William. *Incognita.* edited by H.F.B. Brett-Smith, Houghton-Mifflin, 1922. *Constantia: or, a true picture of human life.* Dublin, 1751.

Craik, Dinah Mulock. "To Novelists—and a Novelist." *MacMillan's Magazine.* April 1861, 441 – 448.

Defoe, Daniel. *Moll Flanders,* edited by David Blewett, Penguin, 1989.

___ . *Robinson Crusoe.* Modern Library, 2001.

Dickens, Charles. *David Copperfield,* Oxford University Press, 1999.

Dunlop, John Colin. *The History of Fiction,* London, 1814.

Eliot, George. "Natural History of German Life." *Westminster Review,* July 1856, pp. 51-56; 71-72.

___ . "Silly Novels by Lady Novelists." *Westminster Review,* October 1856, pp. 442-461.

Fielding, Henry. *Jonathan Wild*. edited by David Nokes, Penguin, 1986.

___. *Joseph Andrews*. edited by Paul O. Scanlon, Broadview Press, 2001.

Fletcher, Andrew. *An Account of a conversation concerning the right regulation of governments for the common good of mankind*. Edinburgh, 1704.

Gisborne, Thomas. *An Enquiry into the Duties of the Female Sex*. 2nd ed. London: T. Cadell and W. Davies, 1797.

Gore, Catherine. "*The Dowager*, or, the New School for Scandal." *The Athenaeum*. November 14, 1840, pp. 899 – 900.

Hazlitt, William. "Mr. Godwin." *The Edinburgh Review*. April 1830, pp. 144 – 159.

Huet, Pierre-Daniel. *The History of Romances*. Translated by Stephen Lewis. London: Hooke and Caldecott, 1715.

Hume, David. "Of the Standard of Taste." *The Rhetorical Tradition: Reading from Classical Times to the Present*. edited by Patricia Bizzell and Bruce Herzberg. Bedford/St. Martin's, 2001.

James, Henry. "The Art of Fiction." *The Critical Muse: Selected Literary Criticism*. Penguin Publishing, 1987, pp. 186-207.

___. "The Future of the Novel." *The Critical Muse: Selected Literary Criticism*. Penguin Publishing, 1987, pp. 335-346.

Johnson, Samuel. *The Lives of the English Poets; and a criticism on their works*. 1780-1781.

___. *The Major Works*. edited by Donald Greene, Oxford UP, 2000.

___. *The Rambler*. vol. 1, no. 4. 1750.

Knox, Vicesimus. *Elegant Extracts in Prose*. 11th ed. London: C. and J. Rivington, et. al., 1824.

Lewis, Stephen. "Preface." *The History of Romances*, Pierre-Daniel Huet. London: Hooke and Caldecott, 1715.

Locke, John. *An Essay Concerning Human Understanding*. London, 1690.

Martineau, Harriet. "Achievements of the Genius of Scott." *Tait's Magazine*. January, 1833, pp. 445 – 460.

Masson, David. *British Novelists and their Styles*. London: MacMillan and Company, 1859.

___. "Inaugural Lecture." (1865). *Studies in Scottish Literature*. vol. 14, 1979, pp. 240-49.

___. "from '*Pendennis* and *Copperfield*: Thackeray and Dickens', *North British Review*." (1851). *Dickens: The Critical Heritage*, edited by Phillip Arthur William Collins, Taylor and Francis, 2003.

___. *Wordsworth, Shelley, Keats, and Other Essays*. London: Macmillan's, 1874.

___. *University of Edinburgh Enrollment Book*. 1865 – 1889. MS Da 35 RHE 2. University of Edinburgh Library, Edinburgh.

___. *Notes of English Literature: From Lectures on Rhetoric and English Literature by Prof. Masson*. 1868 – 1869. MS Gen. 1401 – 1403. University of Edinburgh Library, Edinburgh.

___. *Notes on Professor Masson's Lectures*. 1871 – 1872. MS DK 1.3.2.2. D 6321. University of Edinburgh Library, Edinburgh.

___. *Lectures on English Literature*. 1878 – 1879. MS Gen 2076. University of Edinburgh Library, Edinburgh.

___. *Rhetoric I & English Literature*. 1881 – 1882. MS 6652. National Library of Scotland, Edinburgh.

___. *Rhetoric and English Literature*. 1881 – 1882. MS DK 4.28 – 30. University of Edinburgh Library, Edinburgh.

Morley, Henry. *English Writers: An Attempt Towards a History of English Literature*. New York: Cassell and Company, Ltd., 1887.

Moore, John. "A View of the Commencement and Progress of Romance." *The Work of Tobias Smollett, M.D. with Memoirs of his Life*. London, 1797.

Maginn, William. "Mr. Edward Bulwer-Lytton's Novels; and Remarks on Novel-Writing." *Fraser's Magazine*. June 1830, pp. 509 – 532.

Nimmo, William P., editor. *Episodes of Fiction or Choice Stories from the Great Novelists*. Edinburgh: Balantyne and Company, 1870.

Peacock, Thomas Love. *Nightmare Abbey*, edited by Lisa Vargo, Broadview Editions, 2007.

Plato. *Phaedrus*, in *The Rhetorical Tradition: Readings from Classical Times to the Present*, 2nd ed., edited by Patricia Bizzell and Bruce Herzberg, Bedford/St. Martin's, 2001, pp. 138-169.

Reeve, Clara. *The Old English Baron*. (1778). Oxford UP, 2004

___. *The Progress of Romance*. London, 1785.

Reid, Thomas. *Lectures on the Fine Arts*, edited by Peter Kivy. The Hague: M. Nijhoff, 1973.

Richardson, Samuel. *Pamela; or, Virtue Rewarded*, edited by Peter Sabor, Penguin, 1985.

Saintsbury, George. *A History of English Criticism*. Dodd, Mead, and Company, 1911.

Scott, Walter. "Essay on Romance." *Supplement to the Encyclopedia Britannica*. Edinburgh, 1824.

___. *Notices Biographical and Critical*. Edinburgh, 1820 / 1829.

Smith, Adam. *Lectures on Rhetoric and Belles Lettres,* edited by J.C. Bryce, Liberty Classics, 1985.

Sterne, Laurence. *The Life and Opinions of Tristram Shandy, Gentleman*. Penguin, 1978.

___. *A Sentimental Journey through France and Italy by Mr. Yorick*. Penguin, 2001.

Swift, Jonathan. *Gulliver's Travels*, edited by Robert Demaria, Jr., Penguin Books, 2003.

The Trial: or, the History of Charles Horton, esq. London, 1772.

Walpole, Horace. *The Castle of Otranto*. London, 1764.

Secondary Texts

Adams, Hazard and Leroy Searle, editors. *Critical Theory Since 1965*. Florida State UP, 1986.

Agnew, Lois Peters. *The Art of Common Sense: Victorian Aestheticism and the Rhetorical Tradition*. 1999. Texas Christian University, PhD dissertation.

Altick, Richard. *The English Common Reader: A Social History of the Mass Reading Public, 1800-1900.* University of Chicago Press, 1983.

Armstrong, Nancy. *How Novels Think: The Limits of British Individualism, 1719-1900.* Columbia UP, 2005.

Bakhtin, Mikhail Mikhailovich. *The Dialogic Imagination.* University of Texas Press, 1981.

Bate, Walter Jackson. *From Classic to Romantic: Premises of Taste in Eighteenth Century England.* Harvard UP, 1946.

Bator, Paul G. "The Entrance of the Novel into the Scottish Universities." *The Scottish Invention of English Literature,* edited by Robert Crawford, Cambridge UP, pp. 89-103, 1998.

___ . "Rhetoric and the Novel in the Eighteenth-Century British University Curriculum." *Eighteenth-Century Studies.* vol. 30, no. 2, 1997, pp. 173-196.

Bitzer, Lloyd. "Rhetoric and Public Knowledge." *Rhetoric, Philosophy, and Literature: An Exploration,* edited by Don M. Burks, Purdue UP, 1978, pp. 67-93.

Bizzell, Patricia and Bruce Herzberg. *The Rhetorical Tradition: Readings from Classical Times to the Present.* Bedford / Saint Martin's, 2001.

Brett-Smith, Herbert Francis Brett. "Introduction to *Incognita.*" Houghton-Mifflin, 1922.

Burks, Don M., editor. *Rhetoric, Philosophy, and Literature: An Exploration.* Purdue UP, 1978.

Burwick, Frederick. "Introduction." *Selected Essays on Rhetoric by Thomas De Quincey,* edited by Frederick Burwick, Southern Illinois UP, 1967, xi-xlviii.

Collins, Phillip Arthur William. *Dickens: The Critical Heritage.* Taylor and Francis, 2003.

Crawford, Robert, editor. *The Scottish Invention of English Literature.* Cambridge UP, 1998.

___ . "Introduction." *The Scottish Invention of English Literature,* edited by Robert Crawford, Cambridge University Press, 1998, pp. 1-22.

Davis, Lennard. "Reconsidering Origins: How Novel Are Theories of the Novel?" *Eighteenth-Century Fiction,* vol. 12, no. 2, 2000, pp. 479-499.

Doody, Margaret Anne. *The True Story of the Novel.* Rutgers UP, 1996.

Eagleton, Terry. *The English Novel: An Introduction.* Blackwell, 2004.

Ehninger, Douglas. "Dominant Trends in English Rhetorical Thought, 1750-1800." *Southern Communication Journal,* vol. 18, 1952, pp. 1-16.

Eigner, Edwin M. and George J. Worth. *Victorian Criticism of the Novel.* Cambridge University Press, 1985.

Engell, James. "The New Rhetoric and Romantic Poets." *Rhetorical Traditions and British Romantic Literature,* edited by Don H. Bialostosky and Lawrence D. Needham, Indiana UP, 1995, pp. 217-233.

Ferreira-Buckley, Linda. "The Influence of Hugh Blair's *Lectures on Rhetoric and Belles Lettres* on Victorian Education: Ruskin and Arnold on Cultural Literacy." 1990. Pennsylvania State University, PhD dissertation.

Ferreira-Buckley, Linda and S. Michael Halloran. "Introduction to Hugh Blair's *Lectures on Rhetoric and Belles Lettres.*" Southern Illinois UP, 2005.

Garson, Marjorie. *Moral Taste: Aesthetics, Subjectivity, and Social Power in the Nineteenth-Century Novel.* University of Toronto Press, 2007.

Golden, James L. and Edward P.J. Corbett. *The Rhetoric of Blair, Campbell, and Whately.* Southern Illinois UP, 1990.

___ . "Introduction to *The Rhetoric of Blair, Campbell, and Whately.*" Southern Illinois UP, 1990, pp. 1-18.

Hammond, Brean and Shaun Regan. *Making the Novel: Fiction and Society in Britain, 1660-1789.* Palgrave Macmillan, 2006.

Heidler, Joseph Bunn. *The History, from 1700 to 1800, of English Criticism of Prose Fiction.* University of Illinois Press, 1928.

Horner. Winifred Bryan. "Nineteenth-Century Rhetoric at the University of Edinburgh with an Annotated Bibliography of Archival Materials." *Rhetoric Society Quarterly,* vol. 19, no. 4, 1989, pp. 365 – 375.

___ . *Nineteenth-Century Scottish Rhetoric: The American Connection.* Southern Illinois UP, 1993.

Hunter. J. Paul. *Before Novels: The Cultural Contexts of Eighteenth-Century English Fiction.* W.W. Norton, 1990.

Jauss, Hans Robert. "from *Literary History as a Challenge to Literary Theory.*" *Critical Theory since 1965,* edited by Hazard Adams and Leroy Searle, Florida State UP, 1986, pp. 164-185.

Johnson, Claudia L. "'Let me make the novels of a country': Barbauld's *The British Novelists.*" *Novel: A Forum on Fiction,* vol. 34, no. 2, 2001, pp. 163-180.

Kennedy, George A. *Classical Rhetoric and its Christian and Secular Tradition from Ancient to Modern Times.* University of North Carolina Press, 1999.

Kunitz, Stanley and Howard Haycraft. *British Authors of the Nineteenth Century.* The H.W. Wilson Company, 1936.

Lanham, Richard A. *A Handlist of Rhetorical Terms.* 2nd ed. University of California Press, 1991.

McKeon, Michael. "Generic Transformation and Social Change: Rethinking the Rise of the Novel." *Theory of the Novel: A Historic Approach,* edited by Michael McKeon, Johns Hopkins UP, 2000, pp. 382-400.

___ . "Introduction." *Theory of the Novel: A Historical Approach,* edited by Michael McKeon, Johns Hopkins UP, 2000, pp. xiii-xviii.

___ . *The Origins of the English Novel, 1600-1740.* Baltimore, MD: Johns Hopkins UP, 1987.

___ . "*From* Prose Fiction: Great Britain." *Theory of the Novel: A Historical Approach,* edited by Michael McKeon, Johns Hopkins UP, 2000, pp. 600-613.

McMurtry, Jo. *English Language, English Literature: The Creation of an Academic Discipline.* Archon, 1985.

Miller, Thomas P. *The Formation of College English.* University of Pittsburgh Press, 1997.

Morse, David. *The Age of Virtue: British Culture from the Restoration to Romanticism.* Saint Martin's Press, 2000.

Olmsted, John C. *A Victorian Art of Fiction: Essays on the Novel in British Periodicals, 1830 – 1850.* Garland Publishing, 1979.

Pitcher, Edward. "On the Conventions of Eighteenth-Century Short Fiction: Part I: 1700-1760." *Studies in Short Fiction*. vol. 12, no. 3, 1975, pp. 199-213.

Rhodes, Neil. "From Rhetoric to Criticism." *The Scottish Invention of English Literature*, edited by Robert Crawford, Cambridge UP, 1998, pp. 22-37.

Richetti, John J. "Introduction." *The Cambridge Companion to the Eighteenth-Century Novel*. Edited by John J. Richetti, Cambridge UP, 1998, pp. 1-9.

Robert, Marthe. *The Origins of the Novel*. Bloomington: Indiana UP, 1980.

Ross, Trevor. "Two Ways of Looking at a Canon." *Eighteenth-Century Life*. vol. 21, no. 3, 1997, pp. 90-93.

Sambrook, James. *The Eighteenth Century: The Intellectual and Cultural Context of English Literature, 1700-1789*. New York: Longman, 1988.

Schildgen, Brenda Deen, editor. *The Rhetoric Canon*. Wayne State UP, 1997.

Siskin, Clifford. *The Work of Writing: Literature and Social Change in Britain 1700 – 1830*. The Johns Hopkins UP, 1998.

Sherry, Vincent B. *Joyce: Ulysses, A Student Guide*. 2nd ed., Cambridge UP, 2004.

Spacks, Patricia Meyer. *Novel Beginnings: Experiments in Eighteenth-Century Fiction*. New Haven, Yale UP, 2006.

St. Clair, William. *The Reading Nation in the Romantic Period*. Cambridge UP, 2004.

Stewart, Garrett. *Dear Reader: The Conscripted Audience in Nineteenth-Century British Fiction*. The Johns Hopkins UP, 1996.

Taylor, John Tinnon. *Early Opposition to the English Novel; the popular reaction from 1760 – 1830*. King's Crown Press, 1943.

Uphaus, Robert W. "Jane Austen and Female Reading." *Studies in the Novel*, vol. 19, no. 3, 1987, pp. 334-346.

Warner, William. *Licensing Entertainment: The Elevation of Novel Reading in Britain, 1684-1750*. University of California Press, 1998.

Warnick, Barbara. *The Sixth Canon: Belletristic Rhetorical Theory and Its French Antecedents*. South Carolina UP, 1993.

Watt, Ian P. *The Rise of the Novel: Studies in Defoe, Richardson, and Fielding*. University of California Press, 1957.

Wilson, Hugh. "David Masson." *Nineteenth-Century British Literary Biographers*, edited by Steven Serafin. *Dictionary of Literary Biography*, vol. 144. Detroit: Gale Research, 1994.

White, Hayden. "The Suppression of Rhetoric in the Nineteenth Century." *The Rhetoric Canon*, edited by Brenda Deen Schildgen, Wayne State UP, 1997, pp. 21-31.

Wu. Duncan. *Wordsworth's Reading: 1800-1815*. Cambridge UP, 1995.

Zimmerman, Everett. *The Boundaries of Fiction: History and the 18th-Century British Novel*. Ithaca, Cornell UP, 1996.

Index

A

aesthetics, 5-8, 15, 24, 31, 36, 38, 43-44, 49, 52, 57, 63, 68, 74, 95-97, 101-103, 110
aesthetic theory, 16, 39
  eighteenth-century, 28, 37
  Victorian, 101
Agnew, Lois, 12, 22, 101-102,
Altick, Richard, 8, 48-51, 56, 69
Amelia, 89, 133
Æneid, 96
Apuleius, 74, 112,
Argenis, 98, 131
Aristotle, 53, 88
Armstrong, Nancy, 6, 14,
Arnold, Matthew, 101, 125
Atalantis, 99, 132
Athenaeum, 103
Austen, Jane, 43, 54-56, 124
Aytoun, William Edmondstoune, 119

B

Bain, Alexander, 123
Bakhtin, Mikhail, 13, 25, 27, 37, 111
Ballantyne, John, 99
Barbauld, Anna Laetitia, 8, 53-54, 56, 68, 70-79, 82, 84, 91-93, 95-99, 102, 104, 112, 128, 130
Barrie, James M., 122-123
Barron, William, 122
Bate, Walter Jackson, 26, 28, 60, 69, 79
Bator, Paul, 121-122

Beattie, James, 4, 7, 8, 20, 58, 68-69, 71-81, 87-90, 92-93, 96-99, 112, 122, 130
Behn, Aphra, 3, 25, 30-31, 35, 44, 46, 78, 83-85, 90, 92, 94, 99, 127, 132
belles lettres, 1-3, 5-9, 11-12, 19-23, 36-38, 40-44, 46, 48, 57, 59, 63-66, 67, 74, 76-77, 82, 95-98, 100, 101-104, 107-108, 112-115, 118-119, 121-122, 125-126, 128-129
belletristic rhetoric, 3, 6-7, 9, 12, 21-22, 38, 42-43, 46-48, 57, 60, 63-65, 69-70, 75, 95, 98, 102, 108, 113, 115, 121, 125
bienséance, 38-39, 41-43, 57, 81
Bitzer, Lloyd, 47, 59-60
Bizzell, Patricia, 23, 33, 60, 64
Blair, Hugh, 4, 6-9, 12, 19-23, 47, 58, 60-65, 67-69, 74-75, 77-78, 80, 91, 93, 95-97, 99-100, 102, 114-118, 121-123, 125-126, 127-128, 130
Boileau, Nicolas, 19
Booth, Wayne, 15, 23
Brake, Laurel, 8
Brett-Smith, H.F.B., 39
British Periodicals, 50
British Quarterly Review, 9, 109
Bulwer-Lytton, Edward, 104-105, 129
Bunyan, John, 98, 113, 132
Burke, Edmund, 15, 19, 49, 64-65
Burney, Frances, 45-46, 52-53, 69, 84, 102, 124, 136

C

Caleb Williams, 94, 104, 137

Campbell, George, 4, 19-20, 22, 58, 95, 123, 126
canon
    novel, 8, 66, 68, 70-71, 74, 97-100, 102, 124, 129, 131
    rhetoric, 38, 60, 115
Carlyle, Thomas, 101, 109
Cervantes, Miguel de, 78-79, 98, 112, 131
Clarissa, 19, 31, 85, 88, 92, 94, 116, 129, 133
classical rhetoric, 14, 16, 18-21, 38, 53
cognition, 5, 15-16, 19, 26-29, 38
Collins, Wilkie, 1-3, 5-6, 114
Commencement and Progress of Romance, 71
Congreve, William, 3, 7, 17-18, 25, 30, 35-44, 46, 48, 51, 57, 76-77, 81, 102, 130
Constantia, 50, 53
Corbett, Edward P.J., 22, 63, 95
Cowper, William, 69
Craik, Dinah Mulock, 9, 22, 105-106
Crawford, Robert, 12, 120, 122

D

David Copperfield, 2, 109, 114, 117
Davis, Lennard, 11-12, 42
Defoe, Daniel, 1-2, 4-6, 12-13, 35, 44, 46, 49, 68, 70, 80, 82, 85-86, 90, 99, 113, 116-118, 124, 127, 133
delight, 17, 36-37, 40-41, 43, 51, 73, 77, 85
De Quincey, Thomas, 22-23, 109
development
    of taste, 61, 95
    of taste and judgment, 48, 61

Dickens, Charles, 2-3, 109, 114-115, 117-118, 124, 129
Don Quixote, 2, 78-79, 98, 112, 131
Doody, Margaret Anne, 13, 17, 74
Dunlop, John Colin, 71-77, 79, 82-84, 93-94, 96, 98, 112, 129-130

E

Eagleton, Terry, 13, 17, 84-88, 120
Edgeworth, Maria, 124, 137
Ehninger, Douglas, 18, 21
Eigner, Edwin M., 23, 102-103, 114
Eliot, George, 22, 106-107, 124,
eloquence, 22, 30, 61-62, 88
Engell, James, 4, 20, 23, 27-28, 58
Enlightenment, 7, 16, 26, 32, 38, 80
Essay Concerning Human Understanding, 27, 30
Evelina, or the History of a Young Lady's Entrance into the World, 45, 53, 136

F

fables, 53, 63, 73-75, 80-81, 86, 89
Female Quixote, 99, 133
Fenelon, François, 38-39, 132
Ferdinand, Count Fathom, 94, 134
Ferreira-Buckley, Linda, 21, 60, 63-64, 97, 125
fiction
    amatory, 90
    gothic, 54-56, 82, 94, 99
    literary, 32
Fielding, Henry, 1, 4, 12-13, 35, 43-44, 46, 49, 68, 70, 75, 80, 85-90, 92, 94, 99, 113, 116, 118, 124, 127, 133
five classical canons of rhetoric, 115
Fletcher, Andrew, 67-68, 93

formal realism, 12-13
Fraser's Magazine, 9, 104, 109
French Belles Lettres, 7, 35-36, 38, 40-43

G

Garson, Marjorie, 49
genius, 21, 61, 75-77, 89-92, 95, 98, 100, 102-106, 108, 113-114, 118
Gil Blas, 2, 19, 92, 98, 133
Gisborne, Thomas, 55
Godwin, William, 69, 94, 104, 124, 127, 137
Golden, James L., 22, 63, 95
Goldsmith, Oliver, 69, 94, 109, 124, 127, 134
Gore, Catherine, 103
gothic novels, 55-56
Graff, Gerald, 15, 120

H

Halloran, S. Michael, 21, 60, 63-64, 97
Hammond, Brean, 14, 26, 41-42, 81
Hartley, David, 15, 19
Haycraft, Howard, 109, 121
Haywood, Eliza, 25, 35, 78, 83-84, 90, 99, 133
Hazlitt, William, 22-23, 104
Heidler, Joseph Bunn, 68-69
Herzberg, Bruce, 23, 33, 60, 64
horizon of expectation, 3, 45, 47, 52, 57, 59-60, 63, 65-66, 71, 77, 80, 102-103, 106, 112
Horner, Winifred Bryan, 120-121
Huet, Pierre-Daniel 53
Hume, David, 15, 19, 49, 59-60, 126
Humphrey Clinker, 2, 94, 135

Hunter, J. Paul, 12-14, 24, 25, 34-35, 62, 81,
Hurd, Richard, 68
Hutcheson, Francis, 49

I

imagination, 45-46, 56, 62, 69, 92, 94, 101, 116-117
imaginative fiction, 25, 36-37, 50, 57,
Incognita, 3, 7, 17, 30, 35-44, 48, 57, 77,

J

James, Henry, 8, 22, 111, 125
Jauss, Robert, 47, 65-66
Johnson, Claudia, 68, 70-71, 98
Johnson, Samuel, 35, 51, 54, 77-78, 81, 84, 134
Jonathan Wild, 87, 133
Joseph Andrews, 46, 86-88, 99, 129
Joyce, James, 110, 125
judgment, 4, 8, 15-16, 19-22, 28, 46-49, 51, 54-57, 59-63, 65, 74-76, 89-90, 93-94, 96-97, 99-100, 109, 114, 118, 121-124, 128

K

Keats, John, 126
Kennedy, George A., 21, 27, 33, 38, 96
Knox, Vicesimus, 128
Kunitz, Stanley J., 109, 121

L

Lectures on Rhetoric and Belles Lettres, 8, 19, 21, 59-60, 63-65, 67, 115

letteraturizzazione, 26-27, 37-38, 42
light literature, 114
literacy, 8, 48, 50, 64, 70, 119
literary criticism, 3-4, 8-9, 16, 19, 21-22, 43, 58, 64-65, 100, 108, 120, 123, 125-126
literary history, 2, 4, 47, 109, 113, 124-125
Locke, John, 27-32, 34, 38

M

MacMillan's Magazine, 9, 105, 108-109, 139
Manley, Delarivier, 25, 35, 78, 83-84, 90, 99, 132
Martineau, Harriet, 22, 54, 103-104, 106
Masson, David, 9, 16, 22-23, 100, 101-102, 108-115, 117-119, 122-126, 127, 129-130, 139
Masson, Flora, 139
McClish, Glen, 23
McKeon, Michael, 1, 5, 11, 31-32, 34-35, 50, 53, 59, 63
McMurtry, Jo, 9, 139
middle classes, 48, 105
Miller, D.A., 6
Miller, Thomas P., 15-16, 22, 48-49, 58-59, 63, 71-72, 97, 100, 120
Milton, John, 9, 108-109
Moll Flanders, 86,
The Monk, 54-55
The Moonstone, 1-2, 5-6
Moore, John, 53, 68, 71-77, 79, 81, 92-93, 96, 98, 112, 130
moral purpose, 6, 8-9, 24, 44, 62-63, 65, 93, 103-105, 108, 110-111, 113, 122, 125
Morley, Henry, 16, 23
Morris, William, 101

Morse, David, 43-44

N

narratives, 42, 46, 62, 73, 76, 88, 111
Nichol, John, 121
Nicomachean Ethics, 43
Nightmare Abbey, 56
Nimmo, William P., 127-129
Northanger Abbey, 54-55
novel and romance, 43, 78, 112,
novel canon, 8, 68, 70, 74, 97-98, 100, 129, 131-137
novel histories, 49, 66, 71-72, 74-76, 98, 100, 113, 124
  development of, 49, 71
novelistic discourse, 7, 13-14, 17, 35, 37, 39, 114, 129
novelistic propriety, 105-108

O

Old English Baron, 84
Oliphant, Margaret, 22
Olmsted, John C., 102
oratory, 18-19, 21, 60, 62
Oroonoko, 3, 30-31, 35, 44, 46, 85, 99, 132

P

Pamela, 44, 46, 85, 90, 99, 133
pastoral romance, 79
Pater, Walter, 23
Peacock, Thomas Love, 56-57
Pendennis, 117-118
periodical criticism, 23, 102, 104, 109, 119, 139
periodical press, 7-8, 102, 108, 115
perspicuity, 30, 38, 42-43, 116, 125
Priestley, Joseph, 15, 19-20, 22

probability, 14, 42-43, 46, 57, 65, 75, 77, 80-81, 83, 87-88, 90-93, 95-96, 100, 102-103, 105, 107, 108, 111-112, 114
Progress of Romance, 8, 17, 69, 71-72, 75, 90-91
propriety, 4, 6, 30, 38-43, 51-52, 54, 57, 65, 77, 92, 95-96, 100, 102-103, 105-108, 125, 128

Q

Quarterly Review, 9, 109, 114
Quintilian, 8-9, 16, 18, 21, 60, 64

R

realism, 11-13, 35, 40, 57, 80-88, 92-93, 100, 108, 110-111, 113-114
Reeve, Clara, 8, 17-18, 68-69, 71-79, 81, 84, 89-94, 96-99, 102, 112, 130
Regan, Shaun, 14, 26, 41-42, 81
Regius Chair, University of Edinburgh, 9, 22, 100, 114-115
Reid, Thomas, 15, 19, 59, 126
Restoration, 7, 25-26, 35-37, 43
Rhodes, Neil, 20
Richardson, Samuel, 1, 4, 12-13, 31, 35, 43-44, 46, 49, 68, 70, 84-85, 88, 90, 92, 94, 99, 113, 116, 118, 124, 127-128, 133-134
Richetti, John J., 85, 87-88
Robert, Marthe, 5, 7, 22, 24, 31, 34
Robinson Crusoe, 1-3, 5-6, 12, 19, 35, 44, 46, 80, 82, 90, 94, 99, 116-117, 129, 133
Roderick Random, 2-3, 88, 99, 133
romance
 ancient, 78, 83-84
 historical, 73, 82

medieval, 76, 78, 80, 83, 90, 112
new, 3, 18
prose, 25, 35-36, 53-54, 77, 111
romance conventions, 17, 41
romances and novels, 67, 74-76
romantic period, 20, 47, 57, 64-65, 69
Ross, Trevor, 76, 99-100
Rousseau, Jacques, 46, 68-69, 98, 134
Ruskin, John, 101, 125

S

Saintsbury, George, 16, 22-23, 100
Sambrook, James, 28
Scotland, 12, 49, 99-100, 120, 122, 127
Scott, Walter, 8, 54, 71-79, 82, 94-96, 98-99, 102-104, 106, 112, 124, 128-130, 131
Scottish universities
 eighteenth-century, 15, 95, 120, 122
 nineteenth-century, 120-121
Shakespeare, William, 124
Shelley, Mary, 127
Sheridan, Frances, 84, 91, 99, 134
Sidney Bidulph, 84, 91, 99, 134
Siskin, Clifford, 7-8
sixth canon of rhetoric, 28, 38, 43, 95
Smith, Adam, 4, 20-22, 34, 58-59, 95, 121-122
Smollett, Tobias, 46, 53, 69, 80, 88, 90, 92, 94, 99, 124, 127-128, 133-135
Spacks, Patricia Meyer, 1
St. Andrews University, 20, 122
St. Clair, William, 8, 47, 56-57, 64-65, 69-71, 97,

Sterne, Laurence, 69, 92, 99, 127, 135
Stevenson, Robert Louis, 111
Stewart, Garrett, 46-47
style, 20-22, 38, 57, 60, 62, 84, 95-96, 100, 109, 114-119, 123-125, 128
sublime, 5, 21, 64, 101, 103, 113-114, 116
sympathy, 104-105, 107-108, 121

T

taste, 20-22, 39, 47, 49, 55, 60-62, 69, 71, 74-77, 79-84, 89, 91, 93, 95-98, 100, 103-105, 107-108, 113, 115-116, 121, 128
   and judgment, 4, 8, 15, 16, 19-22, 28, 48-49, 60-63, 74-75, 93, 97, 100, 114, 121-122
Taylor, John Tinnon, 51
Thackeray, William Makepeace, 114, 117-118, 124, 129
Theory of Moral Sentiments, 59
Tom Jones, 2-3, 19, 55, 90, 92, 94, 116, 133
true history, 3, 18, 28, 31
truth and virtue, 32-34, 59

U

Ulysses, 110
University College London, 9, 108-109, 119
University of Aberdeen, 122
University of Edinburgh, 8-9, 63, 67, 95, 100, 108-109, 114, 119, 122, 127, 139
University of Glasgow, 59, 121-122
University of London, 108, 139
Uphaus, Robert, 55

V

verisimilitude, 42, 51, 57, 77, 92, 95, 103-105, 107-108
The Vicar of Wakefield, 2
Victorian criticism, 8-9, 101-103, 114, 125
virtue, 19, 21-22, 26, 31-34, 42-44, 50, 52-54, 56, 59, 62-63, 78, 84-85, 87-97, 100, 112, 115-118, 128,
vraisemblance, 42, 57, 81-82

W

Walpole, Horace, 55-56
Warner, William, 77–78, 193
Warnick, Barbara, 28, 38-39, 42, 74, 95
Watt, Ian, 1, 4, 11-13, 17, 32, 35, 49, 70, 116, 130
Whately, Richard, 95, 123
Wordsworth, William, 69
Worth, George J., 23, 102-103, 114
Wu, Duncan, 15, 65